From the depths of brokenness to the redeeming love of Jesus, Danielle shares her journey on finding healing and shalom peace. Unlock beauty from the ashes of lies and deceit and take heart as you read about a life found in true identity and authority.

— Jenna De Jong, Co-Founder of Action169 and Women's Health Advocate

We had Danielle Freitag at our church and she did an excellent job! Danielle knows her subject, speaks with passion and most importantly, has God's anointing. The Lord is using her in mighty ways!

— Pastor Greg Donnelly, Maple Plain Community Church

Danielle Freitag at her core, is a worshiper of Jesus. The Garden Keys leads you toward *the One* that can heal all wounds and teaches us how to seek Him even more. If you want to feel the presence of God in your reading, this book has been bathed in prayer and it seeps out through the pages.

— Rebecca Bender, CEO & Founder, RBI

The Garden Keys is a must-read for anyone who has dealt with trauma in any form. This book will take you on a journey with King Jesus. The "keys" are imperative for the healing process. It is an encounter of the depths of Father God's love that ministers straight to the heart.

— Sarah Hacker, Hope Encounter Ministries - Minist Healing & Restoration

Danielle's love for Jesus and His living word dances across each page of The Garden Keys and becomes a contagious well of joy to draw from. She not only explains how Jesus has used His Word to transform the most painful experiences of her own life, but she generously offers these keys to the reader, laying them out for all to experience God's healing and redemption.

— KJERSTI BOHRER, SURVIVOR OF COMMERCIAL SEXUAL EXPLOITATION AND FOUNDER OF BEAUTIFUL AND LOVED. AUTHOR, *MY FLAWLESS ONE*

THE GARDEN KEYS

22 KEYS OF RESTORATION, VOLUME 1 - THE
BEGINNING TO ISRAEL

DANIELLE FREITAG

The Garden Keys, 22 Keys of Restoration
Volume 1 - The Beginning to Israel
Copyright ©2018 Danielle Freitag

ISBN: 978-1-945786-02-0

For permission requests, quantity ordering and U.S. trade bookstores please contact the publisher at footprintpub.com or write:
Footprint Publishing, PO Box 1022, Roanoke, TX 76262

Adonai, from the beginning You've made a way to enter into destiny through Truth. You are my Garden.

To my husband, Corey Freitag, thank you for your ongoing love and support. Your love for me is as Christ loves His bride.

To my family, I love you. I am so grateful for each of you. Look at what God has done.

Michael and Jenna De Jong, thank you for your ongoing friendship and support.

Special thanks to you, Anna Friendt. I appreciate you and your talent of creative design that Papa has given you. Thank you for all of your hard work.

Dearest Ruth Schueler, you are to me as Naomi was to Ruth. Thank you for your love, support and knowledge of scripture.

Thank you, Footprint Publishing, for truly walking me through Isaiah 52:7.

May the Lord bless each of you.

Dearest Grace,
Lightning connects us as does Trinity. This cry of longing unites heaven and earth. I love you and long to meet you face to face. Let's keep singing to worship King Jesus.

CONTENTS

FOREWORD

I first met Danielle in the winter of 2008, before she went to South Africa. What struck me about her is that she looked me in the eye. At that first exchange I knew there was something different about her. She could look a stranger in the eye without shame and communicate love that only Jesus gives. At the time I did not know her, but our exchange was not a simple formality. She was eager to talk about how the Holy Spirit was transforming her life.

How a person looks you in the eye can say so much about them. That look told me she was set free from shame and that she had nothing to hide. That being said, this book has been a long time in the making. This book is a product of that purity. This book embodies that direct eye contact that I experienced at that first meeting. Danielle has allowed herself to be completely vulnerable by sharing the struggles and traumas of her childhood and young adult life, while at the same time sharing the keys that set her free and made it possible for her to look me in the eye. I am so grateful for these keys, because without them I would not have a wife and partner in ministry.

For the man considering this, be aware that reading this book will expose the commercial sex industry for what it truly is - a money and power hungry machine that unjustly exploits the vulnerabilities of women. As I have read *The Garden Keys*, my resolve has been strengthened to maintain a purity that allows me to communicate love with a look.

In these pages you will have the opportunity to get to know Danielle. There is not a sentence in this book that was not prayed over nor is there a word that has been wasted. She has poured the last year and a half of her life into this book and has grown so much in the process. If you could receive just a fraction of what she has received while writing this, or what I have by reading it, you will truly be blessed.

Corey Freitag
Action169

INTRODUCTION

Joy and Gladness Will Be Found in You

Indeed, the Lord will comfort Zion; He will comfort all her waste places. And her wilderness He will make like Eden, and her desert like the garden of the Lord; Joy and gladness will be found in her, thanksgiving and sound of a melody.

Isaiah 51:3

Spring, summer, fall and winter of the last several years have been seasons of movement that have shifted us into destiny. Things are moving quickly. There have been both valley and mountaintop moments in these seasons of refining. The places we have walked are all part of a storyline that cause inheritance to manifest in tangible ways. Just as God told Joshua, "Every place on which the sole of your foot treads, I have given it to you" (Joshua 1:3), so too, He is saying to you:

Dear One, before you even acknowledged Me I knew the paths you would take. I have gone before you and made a way for you to enter into all the blessings of inheritance prepared for you on a straight road. I'm calling you out, so that you may come in. You've always been Mine. I knew you would choose love.

The places we have walked, whether moving in recognized covenant with the Lord Jesus Christ or not, can be places of redemption. He knew I would choose love, just as He knew you would choose love. Restoration has always been in the plan.

We've been a part of souls and land entering into already established covenant within the Kingdom of God as designed in the beginning of time. The storyline, including your own, goes back to the beginning - before the garden - and moves forward to the marriage supper of the Lamb, which is another beginning, met with rejoicing and union that will launch us into eternity.

During a summer season on one particular drive home, all I wanted to do was get back to Minnesota. I was returning from a time of learning more about responding to the cry of my heart. Although I was already moving forward in response to the call, I knew someday I would be involved in a training like the one I had just come from. Even though I didn't need anyone's permission to do what God was calling me to do, it helped to get around others who had also come out of the industry and who were now going back for a different purpose.

I was responding to the cry of my heart, which was actually answering the desire of the Father's heart for His daughters - my sisters, already chosen as His inheritance. What remains a constant cry of the heart is for the purpose of fulfilling destiny, and it is not to be ignored.

Through a series of dreams, confirmations and the equipping of a united team, it was time to go back with keys to build a bridge of hope. That strategy blueprint is still being lived out with accompanying signs, wonders and miracles, many of which unfold in the pages of this book.

On our seven-hour drive back from the intensive training, exhaustion took over. Adamant about getting home before the sun came up, I drove through the night. In that season of life, driving for hours in the middle of the night was nothing compared to the late nights, long drives and days of chemically-infused perseverance of the past. My spiritual momma, who was trying to sleep in the passenger seat, woke up a few times through the torrential downpours and never-ending road construction. She must have been praying, because getting back safely was a miracle.

Arriving just as the sun came up, my husband greeted us as we pulled into the driveway. Off my prayer momma went, home to sleep and recover from the days of training.

Once home, I headed through the door and upstairs to my bedroom to catch some much needed sleep. In somewhat of a daze, I quickly drifted off to sleep as the sunshine beamed through the window. In the past, seeing the sun come up meant I had been using and couldn't sleep. This time it was different.

Having slept only an hour, my husband was awakened by the sounds of my uncontrolled sobbing. I had just had an extremely vivid and impactful dream, which was a dream of destiny to write *The Garden Keys*. The dream meant it was time to speak of the miracles I had experienced. It was time to tell of restoration and healing from grief. It was time to write about the commercial sex industry.

God must have been thinking a great deal of His many daughters who have felt some kind of rejection or grief at some time in their life, because the dream also spoke of wounds from childhood yet to be healed.

In the dream, I was back in the strip club. This was the all-too-familiar place that was once like a second home. Back then, I had felt a kind of acceptance in the walls of the club. The people there were like family in some way. In the dream, I was somewhere in a back room, like a dressing room, where I could hear and see two girls fighting. As harsh words spilled forth, I felt the pain as each remark pierced the other's heart.

This pain experienced was from rejection, the deepest kind one could feel. I underwent exactly what this girl was feeling in that moment of dismissal. I had been through this rejection before and I certainly knew the wounds of grief.

The words cut deeply, as harsh words are intended to do. Tears drenched my pillow. I had to get up and pray.

It was the thoughts of these precious ones, their hurts and the Father's heart that brought me to the floor like falling bricks. Much of the weight, tears and thoughts were mixed with memories of my own journey. I knew what it was like in the industry; I had been there for years. I also knew this same kind of dismissal.

While laying on the floor weeping with my eyes closed, I saw many keys falling into my hands. I had to open and close my eyes because the images were so vivid I couldn't tell if it was happening in the physical or spiritual. The gold keys were right there in front of me and so, as an act of receiving them, I held out my hands. The Holy Spirit moved from my head down to my toes like an electric bolt and peace came over me.

Keys of Restoration for the Daughters

Over the course of the next few years, a dream was birthed. Doors of opportunity opened to use the keys on certain occasions as led only by the Holy Spirit and no man. In the pages of this book you will read about some of those miracle moments.

As you read through the stories - the reality moments in the beginning to Egypt, and all the way into the Promised Land - be attentive to your own thoughts. You may remember dreams or have encountering moments. At the end of every chapter there is a devotional section meant for processing what you've read and to embrace its application in your life. Consider keeping a journal to answer the questions and take note of what is revealed to you.

Each chapter of this book has a key of restoration that is already yours. It is my hope that joy and gladness will be found in you as you receive impartations of truth from Holy Spirit as to who you really are.

But you are a chosen people, a royal priesthood, a holy nation, God's special possession, that you may declare the praises of Him who called you out of darkness into His wonderful light. (1 Peter 2:9)

Word of the Year

In the last several years, I have pursued God to receive a word for the year. In 2016, He gave me the word *courage*. Courage is needed to step up, and step out, for all of us. Courage was needed to step out in faith to pursue the dreams that God was calling me towards, and that included taking intentional time to complete this book - a book which began in the places of my childhood.

In December 2016, on a cold Minnesota morning, I sat quietly before the Lord to receive a word for 2017 (Hebrew year 5777). After prayer, spending some time in the Word and sitting still to listen, I heard the soft whisper of Holy Spirit say, "*Garden.*"

That one word triggered a rush of thoughts and memories. I was reminded of the flowers I painted as I learned how to live sober and follow the Lord's leading. I was also reminded that flowers are a gift of spring. I pondered the resilience one single flower could have through various seasons and storms of life. With images imprinted on my mind - colors of blue, green, pink and mauve - I was simultaneously reminded of my favorite movie, *The Secret Garden*.

Time brought me back to the beginning.

Hope stirred deep inside, making all things new - before the violations, the addictions and the greatest heartache I would ever know.

The word for 2018 (Hebrew year 5778) is *esh*, a Hebrew word meaning "fire." Deuteronomy 4:24 teaches us "For the Lord your God is a consuming fire, a jealous God." He loves so deeply that He burns up and cuts off the entanglements in all of our lives in relationship with Him. This is a season of refining and defining the Sons and Daughters of God to draw them back to their first love, Jesus.

The awakening has begun.

May we welcome the refinement of The Lord to, "Awake! Awake!" and "Clothe ourselves with strength!" (see Isaiah 52:1).

In this awakening we will see the signs, wonders and miracles of The Lord, like "All the sons of Israel, seeing the fire come down and the glory of the Lord upon the house" (2 Chronicles 7:3). His glory is manifesting in tangible ways even now. It is my hope and belief that as you read *The Garden Keys* you will experience His presence in deeper ways as deep cries out to deep.

Within each chapter, may you experience a breath of life from Holy Spirit. May revelation understanding of the Father's love for you rise up in your spirit to cause *being seated in Christ* a recognized reality (see Ephesians 2:6, Isaiah 52:2).

Like Zion, may joy and gladness be found in you, as well as thanksgiving and the sound of singing, even when it's difficult to sing. The Lord "...will comfort Zion; He will comfort all her waste places. And her wilderness He will make like Eden, And her desert like the garden of the Lord; Joy and gladness will be found in her, Thanksgiving and sound of a melody" (Isaiah 51:3).

Dear Reader, this is the first of two volumes of *The Garden Keys, 22 Keys of Restoration*. The two volumes are a set that will lead you from the Beginning to Israel, then on to Awakening Daughter Zion.

THE GARDEN
עֵדֶן

1

THE GARDEN

In the beginning God created the heavens and the earth.

Genesis 1:1

At early ages, in the beginning of our lives, my younger sister and I would create exquisite forts. Building was a natural instinct of creativity and our desire for safety played out in the midst of blankets and various colored sheets that we strung together, playing in what was called the *living room*.

The living room was considered the finest room in our three story, Tudor style home near the water. The house had many rooms to play in, and yet this was the room we would build our forts within.

Rarely staying folded and put away for too long, the sheets would be pulled from the upstairs closet as we tried not to draw the attention of our mother, who had taken the time to fold each linen into perfect squares. The thin layers of woven threads would be used to build barricades, shielding off the world outside to create a place of our own.

The large floral cushions from the sofa came in handy for the walls of our secret place. And for the door of our fortress, we would use another of the couch cushions. The floral print came alive as our place of solace was birthed from instinct. Like any secret place, the door was the only way you could enter. The walls kept intruders from coming in while also keeping us safe inside. Looking back, knowing what I do now, it makes sense that we would want our secret place to be in the finest room in the house.

From the very beginning I loved to discover. I was also drawn towards beauty and curiosity. Determination would be strong motive from the start. I exhibited some of the same characteristics of my mother, who over the decades has been quite successful as an antique dealer. Together we have found the most enchanting treasures. Our treasure hunts have taken determination, but it is the relationship itself that is the real treasure, and it inevitably has experienced the pressures of time.

Several of my mom and dad's trinkets and treasures from their travels and generations past were strategically placed on the shelves in this special living room. I vividly remember the large book with gold pages, its white leather cover wrapping words of life in mysteries to be discovered. The book seemed too beautiful to touch and yet, every so often, I would take it off the shelf and flip through the pages while captivated by the edges that shimmered with gold. Although feeling drawn towards searching, I was never sure of what I was looking for. The fine print was too difficult to decipher, so I would place the book with gold-trimmed pages back on the shelf. Although the book was shelved, my story was already a part of the words inside, even in the midst of what was to come. In Psalm 139:16 we read, "Your eyes have seen my unformed substance; and in Your book were all written the days that were ordained for me, when as yet there was not one of them."

Another treasure on the shelf was a gold clock covered in a glass dome. The time clock had a large white face and a few gold bells that would swing from side to side like dancing chimes when it was the right time to move. The clock internally knew the right timing to make a move in the covered safety of the glass dome. This covering protected the special antique that had stood the test of time in my family's lineage. Some things exist protected throughout the generations while other things need to be uncovered.

Also on the shelf in the living room was a large rock that had been split in two. The inside was bright with shades of purple like the color of royalty that looked to my young eyes like diamonds. I was drawn to this particular rock as its colors of light sparkled at just the right angle. If I held the rock to the sunlight near the window, swaying it from side, it would shine brightly when catching the right light.

Amethyst is a mineral gemstone of crystalline purple quartz, which is cut from a bigger rock through various amounts of pressure and time. The rock's name *amethyst* comes from a Greek word meaning "not drunken," and was thought by some to ward off drunkenness and instill a sober and serious mind. The amethyst rock my parents had on their living room shelf was simply there because of its beauty, certainly not because of any thought of deep meaning.

Searching for and collecting rocks has been a generational activity that I would later take great interest in. My great-great-grandma on my mother's side also collected rocks. Her collections were displayed on the shelves of our home, including a high shelf in my mother's closet. If I dragged a chair into the closet and stood up on my tip toes, I could reach for the box of rocks that I loved to sort through.

Directly outside the entrance of the closet was a large dresser with two small drawers on each side. There was a large mirror on top of the dresser and bigger drawers on the bottom for clothes. The right side of the dresser had a small drawer for my mother's things and my father's items were kept on the left. To get into these little drawers I had to maneuver a metal key that didn't really fit into the keyhole, but with a little extra work I was able to get in.

Things became much easier when I was finally shown the right key to use.

What was stored in the small drawers changed over the years and at one point in time I discovered that my mother kept beautiful antique purses along with other trinkets tucked in her small dresser drawer. A few of the small purses became my favorites. Every so often, if I asked nicely, she would let me hold one of them as long as I stayed where she could see me. I can still remember when she moved these tiny beaded purses into her closet, because the collection had grown and would no longer fit inside the small drawer.

After the antique purses, a collection of silver and gold keys filled the drawer. Sure to look for the most unique, most attractive key, I made an effort to go through the small assortment of keys. If there was a *key*, there must be a door; and if there was a door, there must be somewhere worth getting into. I was determined to find that place.

Once I found the right key, if given permission, I would head outside and hide my tiny metal treasure. I knew I had to keep the key safe, because it unlocked something very special. This secret place was what I wanted. At that young age, I never found a secret door other than the ones my sister and I created for our forts. We would pretend these silver and gold keys gave entrance into the forts we built, foretelling things to come.

Treasured places stay hidden only to be discovered by those who search and pursue with honor. Those who are allowed access know that permission comes through covenant.

The Two Became One

For as long as I can remember, my dad has planted small gardens for his family. He loves to be outside to care for the yard and the gardens he has cultivated over the years. He enjoys seeing the outcome of his labor. Not only does he find fulfillment in the work, but he loves knowing his family can enjoy what comes from the garden, whether flowers and plants that are pleasant to the eyes or vegetables and fruits that nourish the body.

He's been a hard worker who took on a family business with his brother and sister. Passed down from his father, the business has lasted through the years. My dad has portrayed the characteristics of a son of God to design, build, protect and persevere.

My mom and dad were both 22 years old when they came into covenant to be married on September 11, 1971 (9-11). A union of this length takes years of perseverance as well as the miracles told of in these pages. They were married for just about twelve years without having children. In fact, they were in the process of adoption when they found out they were pregnant with me. Because they thought I was going to be a boy, they had the name Daniel picked out, but God had a different plan and the name Danielle was preserved.

There is a time, purpose and reason for all things, including pregnancy, names, birthdate and gender. In the book of Psalms the psalmist declares of God, "For You formed my inward parts; You wove me in my mother's womb" (Psalm 139:13).

Seeing photos of my mom and dad newly married and so in love has always brought joy. The way my mom would look at my dad is how I wanted to someday look at my husband. My dad had curly brown hair that resembled the baby boomer generation of hippies and love. My mom, a young woman in the 60's and 70's, had long brown hair and the fun clothing of the times. For their wedding she had the most beautiful white dress. Standing in a rose garden under the canopy of a blue sky she wore a crown of flowers that matched the floral theme of their wedding where they united in covenant for life.

Gardens have always been in the storyline, and so has covenant.

Gardening is something that my dad has taught his grandson, my sister's son. He taught him that in the spring the soil becomes perfect for planting seeds. The sky produces rain and later the sun gives its warmth to coax tiny buds to emerge through the soil. In the garden two can work together, each learning from the other.

Although I've always loved flowers and gardens, I did not

receive the green thumb gift that my dad has. It is possible the gift is buried somewhere deep inside and I just haven't taken the time to cultivate it yet. I have planted one flower in my existence that has actually budded and remained through the years - the beautiful rose bush outside our home that has added color to our otherwise drab yard. Each year this magnificent rose bush grows bigger by blossoming with many strong roses.

Garden of Eden

The garden in Eden, as spoken of in the book of Genesis, was full of life. There was surely more than one beautiful rose bush. This garden contained lush vegetation including fruit, trees and flowers in an array of colors pleasing to the senses. Beauty blossomed where there was no shame, which tells us that God appreciates beauty and made us to regard beauty as well. The description of the garden leaves no question as to the extravagance of God's perfect paradise created for the ones He loves.

Eden is a vision of the world in its perfect state. In fact, the word *eden* means "delight."

In the beginning, there was intimacy in a place of delight with no shame or grief and no knowledge of death or destruction. In the garden, there was creativity to cultivate and meet with God face to face.

Adama is the Hebrew word for "earth." God formed the first man, Adam, from the dust of the earth and filled him with a breath of life. Then, God planted a garden in Eden for Adam to tend to and enjoy cultivating. While the garden was indeed an extravagant place of delight, it was not yet perfect for Adam because there was no helper fit for him. The final jewel in the crown was still missing.

Then the Lord God said, 'It is not good for the man to be alone; I will make him a helper suitable for him.' (Genesis 2:18)

So the Lord God caused a deep sleep to fall upon the man, and he slept; then He took one of his ribs and closed up the flesh at that place. The Lord God fashioned into a woman the rib which He had taken from the man, and brought her to the man. The man said, "This is now bone of my bones, and flesh of my flesh; She shall be called Woman, because she was taken out of Man." For this reason a man shall leave his father and his mother, and be joined to his wife; and they shall become one flesh. And the man and his wife were both naked and were not ashamed. (Genesis 2:21-25)

What and who God gave to man, man was to be responsible for in relationship to God. The garden needed care, and so did the woman, the jewel in the crown that had been created from Adam's rib. Adam and Eve were meant to live with God in perfect union, created in His image and destined to fill the earth and cultivate the ground which was given to them in the garden.

God created man in His own image, in the image of God He created him; male and female He created them. God blessed them; and God said to them, "Be fruitful and multiply, and fill the earth, and subdue it; and rule over the fish of the sea and over the birds of the sky and over every living thing that moves on the earth." (Genesis 1:27-28)

The word *subdue* means "to cultivate, conquer, and bring into subjection." Adam and Eve were meant to subdue the earth. God had placed them in the garden to learn to cultivate that which was given to them.

People in previous generations have viewed gardens differently than we do now. Those of royalty had large gardens that people would walk through and enjoy. It could take an entire day just to see and appreciate each flower. Gardens were associated with royalty and divinity. Today, many of us have become accustomed to smaller gardens that can be seen in the blink of an eye. While they are beautiful, they are much smaller in comparison.

In Genesis 3:8 God is described as walking in the garden in the cool of the day. I wonder if He wanted to see the flowers He created? He surely delighted to share such beauty with His beloved ones, the ones He created and desired to be with. The garden was His dwelling place, and His first temple on earth. In this temple He met face to face with the ones He created. The environment was a perfect state of harmony where man, woman and animal coexisted without death or threat. God's handiwork, delightful in every sense, made no room for separation between the physical and the spiritual.

From the beginning, intimacy was designed to be untainted and without shame. Eden was the perfect home for man and woman to fulfill the very first mandate to be fruitful and increase in number, which meant their sexual union would be one without any shame or violation.

This perfect place was interrupted when, in a moment and acting out of free will, curiosity was influenced by whispers of the deceiver. Both Adam and Eve ate fruit of the tree which God had told them not to eat. This first act of disobedience was no surprise to God, as He had already devised a plan of redemption through His Son. In fact, the Bible tells us that before the foundation of the world names were written in the Lamb's *Book of Life* (see Revelation 13:8 and Psalm 139:16).

Once the fruit was eaten, the couple knew they were naked. Feeling exposed, they felt they had to hide from God and so they covered themselves. Now their safe and secret place would no longer be a place of direct communication with God, but because communion, covering and covenant have always been important, a plan had already been constructed to clothe and cover in covenant the ones created for communion.

He did not want them to also eat from the other tree, so after God clothed them with garments the couple was driven out of the garden. We read in Genesis 3:24 that the garden is now being guarded by cherubim and a flaming sword.

Communion with someone I could connect with and covering

within the walls of a secret place has been a determination from the beginning. These are things all of us have internally longed for from the start as designed by our Creator Himself. *Covenant*, also known as "agreement or commitment to relationship," has shown itself through my life for both good and bad. Thankfully, His covenant with me was always stronger to bring me back to my first love.

The covenant God made with Abraham, the father of our faith, applies to both you and me. In Genesis, God speaks to Abraham, saying:

> I will make you exceedingly fruitful, and I will make nations of you, and kings will come forth from you. I will establish My covenant between Me and you and your descendants after you throughout their generations for an everlasting covenant, to be God to you and to your descendants after you. I will give to you and to your descendants after you, the land of your sojournings, all the land of Canaan, for an everlasting possession; and I will be their God. (Genesis 17:6-8)

Determined

My obsession with keys came after seeing my favorite of all childhood movies, *The Secret Garden* (the Hallmark Hall of Fame version). The mystery and attraction of discovering a secret place that was safe and secure, only to be shared with those I trusted, was the love story I always wanted to unlock.

The movie was created long after the book it was based on was released. The book *The Secret Garden*, written by Frances Hodgson Burnett, was first published in 1911. It was a walled garden called the Great Maytham Hall that provided the inspiration for this most famous book for children. Burnett wrote with words that were divinely inspired. I believe she was a woman who walked closely with God. She must have understood the power of keys and the garden. She certainly had insight into the blessing God gives when we walk in love.

Mary Lennox, the story's main character, knew that if there was a key, there would be a door. She was determined to find the key to enter into the secret garden she'd heard about. Some people had told her the garden was off limits. Others said it was non-existent all together. Those close to her told her she would never find the garden. She was told to forget about it but the words and actions of others never stopped her from pursuing what she knew was worth pursing. Mary knew there was a safe place where flowers would bloom with loving care.

Only when she found the key was she able to gain access to the garden through the door. Once little Mary discovered the key and the garden door, she hid them both saying, "It's my garden now, my own secret garden," and yet, she was not able to keep the discovery to herself for very long. Mary knew the garden would cause joy and healing for others and so she extended the invitation for others to come in. Some of her very own family came back to the garden where they had once experienced miracles of their own.

The garden, once blooming with life, had been closed up after overwhelming grief was felt from the separation of a loved one. Mary's uncle was sick with grief from the death of his bride who had fallen from a branch in the garden. He had decided that if the garden could not be enjoyed together with his beloved, then it would be shut up. After closing the garden and never dealing with his grief, it wasn't until Mary came along that hope was discovered. A dream of his cherished companion in their beautiful garden awakened him to go back into the garden.

Because of his niece Mary and the work she put into the garden, he was able to walk back into the garden and find healing from his grief. The loss of his loved one was still with him. He would never forget the love he felt for her, but now he was able to enjoy life once again.

Mary's determination and dreams of the garden gave hope.

As a child imitating my favorite love story, I hid my own key within the brick walls of my dad's neatly kept garden. In my imagination, I believed there was a door somewhere that my key would unlock.

Little did I know, this hidden key would later resemble the keys that would open the door to allow healing where my song had been stolen.

> Therefore, behold, I will allure her, bring her into the wilderness and speak kindly to her. Then I will give her her vineyards from there, and the valley of Achor as a door of hope. And she will sing there as in the days of her youth, as in the day when she came up from the land of Egypt. (Hosea 2:14-15)

Achor means "trouble." The grief and shame of exposure and violation brought me into a valley of trouble. Even so, determination would give hope and dreams would light the way to freedom. There are moments in childhood that can introduce us to our destiny and hiding that metal key in a garden wall was a destiny moment for me.

In the heart of every little boy and girl there is a desire to search, discover and ask questions. I soon learned that there were things on the other side of curiosity that I didn't really want to know. Like all of us, I learned about good things as well as bad, or evil things. There was a pull on my young mind towards what was good, yet there was also a distraction that led me into harm. In a journal I recorded at a young age, I once described this inner conflict as a battle within. We've all felt this battle in one way or another.

When the apple was eaten, their eyes were opened and Adam and Eve knew of both good and evil. They felt exposed the moment they ate the apple, which we know because they immediately sewed fig leaves together to cover themselves. They felt they had to hide from God, yet God knew what they had done and even made them coverings before having them leave the garden.

This story raises so many questions: Why put the tree of the knowledge of good and evil within reach? Didn't God know His children would eat the fruit? Isn't God all-knowing?

Of course He is all knowing and He knew exactly what Adam and Eve would do. Nothing is a surprise to an all-knowing God.

Each of us is truly lovesick for Eden, that place of intimacy with God. In Ecclesiastes 3:11 we are told that, "Eternity has been set in our hearts." From the start, determination has been moving through our veins to bring us into the garden. To understand the storyline, the defeat of the deceiver and the victory that is already ours, we must first find the door and utilize the keys we have been given.

With hope and determination, Mary Lenox found her secret garden. As a result, her loved ones would reap the benefits of her discovery. Despite going through grief from loss she found love in a rose garden.

BEGINNING KEY

1. What trinkets and treasures were significant to you in the beginning years of your childhood?

2. What did you like to create when you were young? Write and share about any forts or places of covering that you built.

3. What good memories do you have of your childhood?

4. When was a time you felt like you had to hide?

5. What were some things you were determined to do when you were young?

6. Read Genesis 1 and 2. What happened in the beginning?

2

JOSEPH THE DREAMER

And God sent me before you to preserve for you a remnant on earth, and to keep alive for you many survivors. So it was not you who sent me here, but God.

Genesis 45:7 ESV

When Joseph's brothers saw him coming, they recognized him in the distance. As he approached, they made plans to kill him.

> They said to one another, "Here comes this dreamer! Now then, come and let us kill him and throw him into one of the pits; and we will say, 'A wild beast devoured him.' Then let us see what will become of his dreams." (Genesis 37:19-20)

Joseph certainly had challenging family times. His life story is seeped with plenty of moments he could have lived in offense, yet Joseph chose a better way. There was something unusual about

Joseph, just like there is something unusual about those who rise up despite the attempts of others to sabotage.

Dream killers will quickly recognize a dream to be tampered with. They are out there and they can be vicious to try and stop the destinies of those who dream. The good news is that even though the dream killers are out there, there are also real heroes among us who keep going despite the actions of others.

Joseph was one of those heroes and his story is worth visiting.

Joseph the dreamer experienced the dismissal and rejection of his own brothers who harbored jealousy and hate towards him. Imagine for a moment, the feelings of rejection that would accompany your own family members plotting to take you out.

He became a target within his own household.

The name *Joseph* means "God shall add," and he was the second youngest of 12 brothers. He may have had more than one sister, but scripture tells us for sure that he had a sister named Dinah. His father Jacob (later named Israel) was married to both Leah and Rachel, who were sisters.

Joseph actually had ten half brothers and one full brother who was named Benjamin. Benjamin was Joseph's youngest brother, also the son of Jacob's beloved Rachel. Things may have been different back in biblical times, but it has always been God's heart for one man and one woman to unite and become one flesh as was orchestrated in the garden. Every attempt of the snake since he deceived Eve in the garden has been against the first mandate found in Genesis 1:28, "Be fruitful and multiply and fill the earth and subdue it."

Carrying on the family lineage has always held great significance.

Jacob worked diligently for seven years with the hope and the assurance that he could marry Rachel, Laban's daughter. In Genesis 29:20, we read, "Jacob served seven years for Rachel, and they seemed to him but a few days because of the love he had for her." Jacob chose love in the midst of difficult times, and the process was but a moment for him.

Although Laban agreed to give his daughter Rachel in marriage to Jacob, he tricked Jacob and substituted his other daughter Leah on the supposed wedding night union of Jacob and Rachel. Jacob found out he had been tricked and still he chose to labor another seven years to marry Rachel! What an amazing picture he displayed of patient love.

For a total of 14 years Jacob was lovesick for his bride.

Jacob labored out of a place of longing. He chose to forgive even though he could have harbored great anger towards Laban. He also could have chosen to give up, but the love he had for his bride was great, so he kept on going. Had Jacob given up, the twelve tribes of Israel would be non-existent. Even after marrying Rachel, Jacob worked for Laban for another seven years to build a flock of his own to provide for his family.

Once Rachel became Jacob's wife, babies followed, but not until after a season of barrenness. Both sisters Leah and Rachel offered their maidservants to Jacob during their own times of barrenness. Like these women, we too can become eager for the promise, but we must not miss what a season of waiting can produce. It is often in the pain of crying out in barrenness that destiny is birthed.

For the sake of context, let's look at the order in which the brothers were born and whether they were born to Leah, Rachel or their concubines. The eldest to the youngest boys in the family as found in scripture are:

- Reuben - Son to Leah (Genesis 29:32)
- Simeon - Son to Leah (Genesis 29:33)
- Levi - Son to Leah (Genesis 29:34)
- Judah - Son to Leah (Genesis 29:35)
- Dan - Son to Bilhah, Rachel's maidservant (Genesis 30:4-6)
- Naphtali - Son to Bilhah, Rachel's maidservant (Genesis 30:7-8)
- Gad - Son to Zilpah, Leah's maidservant (Genesis 30:10-11)

- Asher, Son to Zilpah, Leah's maidservant (Genesis 30:12-13)
- Issachar, Son to Leah (Genesis 30:17-18)
- Zubulun, Son to Leah (Genesis 30:20)
- Joseph, Son to Rachel (Genesis 30:23-24)
- Benjamin, Son to Rachel (Genesis 30:22-24)

These sons of Jacob made up the twelve tribes of Israel, except that Levi was not included in that list. The Tribe of Levi would be set apart as priests and receive the inheritance of the Lord, but not the land. And in the place of Joseph the list of tribes would include his two sons, Manasseh and Ephraim.

Of Jacob's daughters, only Dinah is mentioned by name.

Each of Jacob's sons and daughters were once young with hopes and dreams. Along the way, anger and jealousy motivated some to take actions that choked life from those who breathed deeply with hope. Once acted upon, anger led to revenge which grew like weeds. And so, when the vision of a dream was shared, there was an attempt to destroy it from the start.

Joseph had vivid dreams that he recanted to his family in great detail. The dreams were meant to shape the course of his life but they angered his brothers to the point of taking extreme measures. Those extreme measures included the terrible plan to kill him that we read about in Genesis 37.

Before there was a plot to destroy Joseph and his dreams, there was a gift. That gift would set the course of history for this family and bring direction for the Israelites in a time of famine. Despite the dream killers both within and outside of Joseph's own family, a powerful story of redemption and love had already been written.

The dreams with all their twists and turns actually had a ripple effect that positively influenced a nation.

You see, the dreams weren't necessarily all about Joseph, but about all those in his lineage as well as those he would meet over the course of his life. His story would be one that pointed solely to the God of miracles who had it all figured it out from the start.

· · ·

The Robe of Many Colors

Jacob, Joseph's father, had made known his love for His son with a foretelling gift of inheritance. We read:

> Israel loved Joseph more than any of his sons, because he was the son of his old age. And he made him a robe of many colors. (Genesis 37:3 ESV)

Another name for this robe is a *septuagint*, meaning "a robe with long sleeves." The Hebrew phrase *kethoneth passimm*, which is the Hebrew term for "robe," is translated here as "coat of many colors."

In Joseph's day, almost everyone had a coat or a robe of some kind, but at that time most would have been very plain. These cloaks served many purposes including keeping warm, carrying belongings and even serving as security for a loan. In contrast to the common cloaks of the age, the coat Jacob gifted his son was colorful, ankle length and resembled what royalty would wear.

Imagine a 17 year old boy who pastured sheep, the second youngest of his brothers, wearing a cloak of royalty. Let's be honest here, I know if my mom or dad gave my sister something of great value when we were young I could have had some negative feelings that accompanied that gift. In the case of Joseph's brothers, "His brothers saw that their father loved him more than all his brothers; and so they hated him and could not speak to him on friendly terms" (Genesis 37:4).

The coat was a token of his fathers great love and recognition, yet, along with the coat came the envious brothers who let the poison of jealousy seep into their hearts. In addition to that robe of many colors, Joseph was also given a few other gifts that would shape the course of his life. Gifts have a tendency to do that.

· · ·

The Dream

Joseph was gifted with dreams that revealed the plans of God. Those dreams did not come from Joseph's own efforts, but by the Spirit of God who was with him. The God who gave Joseph dreams revealing His divine plans is the same God who gives dreams to His sons and daughters today.

The dream that shaped Joseph's life was also the dream that brought difficult times. Joseph boldly declared to his brothers:

> Please hear this dream which I have dreamed: There we were, binding sheaves in the field. Then behold, my sheaf arose and also stood upright; and indeed your sheaves stood all around and bowed down to my sheaf. (Genesis 37:7 NKJV)

Joseph's brothers were not at all pleased with the dream their brother had just described. His brothers said to him, "Are you actually going to reign over us? Or are you really going to rule over us?" (Genesis 37:8). Bowing down to their brother wasn't something they had on their list of things to do.

Joseph had yet another dream. He told his brothers, "I have had still another dream; and behold, the sun and the moon and eleven stars were bowing down to me" (Genesis 37:9).

After sharing this vision with his brothers and father, his father rebuked him for thinking the family would bow down to Joseph. His brothers harbored resentment toward him over this strange dream but his father kept this saying in his mind.

God came to Joseph in this dream to reveal his plan for Joseph's life. Joseph didn't really know at this point exactly what this dream entailed. Initially, when we have a dream that initiates vision and direction for life it can be a challenge to think of how that dream will be fulfilled. Yet, when we are given God-given dreams, it is God Himself who works out the fulfillment of the dreams within our lives, just as He did with Joseph. Joseph was already included in the covenant God made with Abraham before this moment of dismissal from his brothers.

Joseph didn't know where this dream would lead him or how it would develop within the storyline of his life. What he did right was keep his focus as the dream literally took him from the pit to the palace.

The Pit to the Palace

The garment and the dream, one a gift from his earthly father and the other from his heavenly Father, created temporary tough times for Joseph.

> So it came to pass, when Joseph had come to his brothers, that they stripped Joseph of his tunic, the tunic of many colors that was on him. Then they took him and cast him into a pit. And the pit was empty; there was no water in it. (Genesis 37:23-24 NKJV)

While Joseph was in a place that was desolate and dry, I'm sure he sought comfort from the one who gave him the dream. Alone in the bottom of a well, left to die with no water, anger would do nothing to get him out. Survival mode kicked in to trigger his fight or flight instinct. There is no further account of what happened to Joseph in that pit. I wonder what thoughts, prayers or divine encounters occurred?

Whatever thoughts he wrestled with, there was more to the story.

On the other side of the desolate pit, there was a palace experience waiting for Joseph that came with a great purpose of destiny.

Not everything is as it seems.

A few of Joseph's brothers refrained from harboring vicious intent to betray and destroy their brother. First, Reuben persuaded his brothers not to shed Joseph's blood. Then Judah made sure to make a get-away plan for Joseph. There came a window of opportunity for Joseph to escape the pit he had been tossed into.

It is very possible that guilt started to settle in for his brothers as they realized what they had done. While their brother Joseph was still nearby, likely crying out for help while left in the pit to die, his brothers saw a caravan of Ishmaelites on their way to Egypt.

> Judah said to his brothers, "What profit is it for us to kill our brother and cover up his blood? Come and let us sell him to the Ishmaelites and not lay our hands on him, for he is our brother, our own flesh." And his brothers listened to him. Then some Midianite traders passed by, so they pulled him up and lifted Joseph out of the pit, and sold him to the Ishmaelites for twenty shekels of silver. Thus they brought Joseph into Egypt. (Genesis 37:26-28)

Joseph was then taken to the foreign land of Egypt, the place of his captivity.

After the tragic trade, the brothers lied to their father about what really happened. Joseph's robe, which they had stripped off him and dipped in the blood of a goat, was the false evidence that was used to convince their father that Joseph had been killed.

Jacob's heart was broken. His grief would not be consoled. His very own sons lied to him about his beloved Joseph. Jacob had lost his beloved wife Rachel, his father Isaac, and now he lived with the pain of losing his son Joseph. Little did he know, his son Joseph was about to be elevated to a place of royalty - from a pit to a palace.

Joseph the dreamer was sold as a slave into the land of Egypt for 20 shekels.

His brothers had been swayed by toxic emotions of jealousy to do what was evil. Yet, God never left Joseph, and instead He gave him favor that later brought redemption to the very ones who tried to take him out.

Joseph was brought to Egypt and purchased by a man named Potiphar, who was an officer in Pharaoh's court. Joseph quickly found success working under Potiphar. His master took notice of his dedication and hard work and decided to put Joseph in charge of everything in his house. For some years Joseph continued in the house of Potiphar. He may have been a slave in name, but in reality he was the master of all of Potiphar's affairs.

One day Potiphar's wife took notice of Joseph and tried to seduce him. Joseph desperately attempted to fend her off, but when they were alone, "She caught him by his garment, saying, 'Lie with me!' And he left his garment in her hand and fled, and went outside" (Genesis 39:12). Potiphar's wife showed the garment to her husband and accused Joseph of trying to lie with her. Potiphar falsely concluded by looking at Joseph's garment that Joseph was guilty of wanting to lie with his wife. Immediately, Joseph was taken to prison and once again, tossed aside.

Joseph Interprets the Dream

Even though Joseph was thrown into another place of confinement, his dreams of destiny were still alive. God gave Joseph favor in the sight of others, including the warden, who put Joseph in charge of all that went on in the prison. That promotion positioned Joseph to interpret the dreams of two of Pharaoh's officers who had been thrown in jail. Those in the jail quickly noticed that there was something different about Joseph.

After both of the dream interpretations were given, the officers were brought back into Pharaoh's court.

> Thus it came about on the third day, which was Pharaoh's birthday, that he made a feast for all his servants; and he lifted up the head of the chief cupbearer and the head of the chief baker among his servants. He restored the chief cupbearer to his office, and he put the cup into Pharaoh's hand; but he hanged the chief baker, just as Joseph had interpreted to them. (Genesis 40:20-22)

Two full years went by, and it was not until Pharaoh was disturbed by his own troubling dreams that the chief cupbearer was reminded of his shortcoming of forgetting about Joseph. Even though some may forget or neglect to give credit, God is the one who sees and elevates His sons and daughters.

Joseph could have lost faith and became bitter, and yet he did not harden his heart. The Lord was with him even in the darkest of times, showing him kindness and granting him favor in the eyes of those who sought to bring him harm, whether by accusation, confinement or being forgotten.

Eventually, Joseph is remembered and brought out of prison to interpret Pharaoh's dreams. No other person in all of Pharaoh's court was able to correctly interpret the dream, so Joseph's gift earned him a royal seat. Once again, he went from the pit to the palace, free of blame, shame or cursing anyone's name.

Fruitful in the Land of Troubles

After rising from a slave to Pharaoh's most trusted aide, Joseph saved Egypt from seven years of famine. He had a willing spirit of service and was able to do anything he put his hand too. He worked diligently as he had when he pastured the flock as a young man. He saw that the earth was abundant to produce grain, so for seven years he stored up in every city the food grown in the fields surrounding it. Joseph also taught the people to not be wasteful, but to save the food for the coming time of need. Pharaoh's dream that Joseph interpreted foretold of a lean season coming on the horizon.

Joseph and his wife Asenath, the daughter to the king of Egypt, named their first of two sons *Manasseh*, a word that meant "making to forget." They named their next son *Ephraim*, which meant "fruitful," because God has made Joseph fruitful in the land of his affliction. After the seven years of plenty passed, there was great need in the region, but not in the land of Egypt, thanks to Joseph.

The Family Redemption

Life continued back in Joseph's childhood home. His brother

Judah had matured greatly, showing honesty and unprecedented accountability for his actions (see Genesis 38:26). He even chose to protect his father and youngest brother at a time when he had could have chosen otherwise.

This willingness to lay down his life for his family foreshadowed the sacrifice of Jesus Christ. And so, like King David and Solomon before Him, Jesus descended from Judah and the Judaic linage of love, redemption, and prophetic praise first spoken through their foremother, Leah, whom God blessed and loved.

One day, when the famine was so severe that it had even reached Joseph's family who lived outside of Egypt, Judah and the brothers traveled to the palace hoping to receive help. They had no idea of the surprise that awaited them.

When they arrived in Egypt they came face-to-face with their long lost brother, but they did not recognize him. At first, Joseph spoke roughly with his brothers. He improvised a lesson and time of testing for some of his brothers. Through the testing and a blessing that Joseph provided for them, compassion grew in his brothers' hearts. Eventually, Joseph revealed himself out of longing for the nearness of his brothers, especially Benjamin.

Joseph had nothing but love for his brothers. He knew that if it weren't for his position in Egypt, his family could have very well died from the famine. Joseph said, "You intended to harm me, but God intended it for good to accomplish what is now being done, the saving of many lives" (Genesis 50:20 NIV). Joseph's brothers fell upon their faces before him, just as he had been shown in the dream.

Forgiveness, for Joseph, was greater than vengeance. Compassion, more powerful than anger. And Israel, the father who had mourned, was comforted in the embrace of his son once again.

A miracle of reunification is always a part of the storyline when forgiveness and love are chosen.

It was never a surprise to God that Joseph would go through troubling times. While Joseph experienced the vile attempts of a deceiver, love won anyway! Love will always win.

Joseph had to have known, because of His relationship with God, that love would be more powerful than hate. Even so, his faith was challenged in numerous ways. Joseph's triumphant story gives understanding and hope to those of us who have felt pain, betrayal, forgotten or even tempted.

An American clergymen by the name of William Ellery Channing once said that, "No power in society, no hardship in your condition can depress you, keep you down, in knowledge, power, virtue, or influence, but by your own consent."[1]

In spite of being sold as a slave, thrown into prison, forgotten, laughed at and accused, Joseph never consented with these harsh actions, nor did he choose to be influenced by the feelings that could accompany such treatment.

Of course, there may have been moments when Joseph felt angry, but overall, the scriptures indicate that he exhibited exceptional character during times of trial. For example, he showed grace towards his brothers even when they sold him into slavery. Jospeh also displayed faithfulness to God, never wavering from his commitment to follow Him, even when he was thrown into jail for a crime he did not commit.

Joseph chose love because Love had chosen him, and just like you and me, Joseph was created in such a way that he could make his own choices.

He chose not to be angry. His brothers also had free will to choose what they would allow to take root in their thoughts.

We each have a choice.

The Attempt Understood

In Genesis 46, God speaks to Israel, telling him that he does not need to be afraid to go to Egypt to be with his son Joseph and the rest of his family who would sojourn the foreign land. Israel is assured that if he goes to Egypt, God would go with him and bring him out again. He is assured of being fruitful and multiplying in the land.

It is by understanding what happened in Joseph's life, his dream and the dream of his father Jacob, that we can understand the storyline and the attempt of evil to bring destruction. Evil's attempt is to battle with the first mandate and bring question against the One who gave it.

Remember, the Genesis 1:28 mandate given to Adam and Eve was to, "Be fruitful and multiply and fill the earth and subdue it." The snake whispered into Eve's ear, bringing question to what God said, while seeking to appeal to her senses. Once the choice was made to believe deception instead of truth, hiding came naturally.

Like his son Joseph and those to come, Jacob (Israel) was also a dreamer with destiny living in his veins. Destiny brings us into covenants already made by our Creator, just as destiny did with Joseph and his father.

In Jacob's dream, he saw a stairway resting on the earth with its top reaching to heaven, and the angels of God were ascending and descending in movement:

And behold, the Lord stood above it and said, 'I am the Lord, the God of your father Abraham and the God of Isaac; the land on which you lie, I will give it to you and to your descendants. Your descendants will also be like the dust of the earth, and you will spread out to the west and to the east and to the north and to the south; and in you and in your descendants shall all the families of the earth be blessed. Behold, I am with you and will keep you wherever you go, and will bring you back to this land; for I will not leave you until I have done what I have promised you. (Genesis 28:13-15)

Let's be sure we explicitly understand that evil's attempt is to:

- Bring question to what God said (Genesis 3:1)
- Bring deception to put to test what God said, speaking in complete opposition of truth (Genesis 3:4)
- Appeal to the senses, sometimes for power (Genesis 3:6)

Cutting off mankind and creating the feeling of shame that comes with being deceived was and still is evil's attempt. Just like Adam and Eve, feeling the need to hide is what many of us have done at different times in our lives when we internally know something isn't right. The snake did not want Adam and Eve to multiply and have children or to enjoy one another without shame, so he brought deception. These were the very ones made in God's image with purpose and a destiny to subdue the earth, just like Joseph and his lineage.

Thankfully, there is more to the story to bring about restoration and victory. There is already a happy ending, and that is just the beginning.

Stripped of My Robe

Stripped of my robe, I experienced moments of violation, betrayal, poor choices and seduction that forced, coerced and allured me into forms of slavery in the years to come. The pit would be dark, even though it appeared like a light for awhile.

The dreams that were given to me when I was a little girl seemed to become like dust in the wind. Like anyone who wrestles with destiny, I faced times of pain, loss, and betrayal.

Just a day in a hundred years, was the moment that Joseph was sold into slavery.

Just a day in a hundred years, was the moment I acted in agreement to a form of control.

Young in age and under the influence of what would ultimately bring grief and years of exploitation, captivity took hold and bound me in invisible chains. With a secret to be kept, substances seemed to bring relief and the seduction of the sex industry appeared, for a while, like a solution to some kind of longing.

In the case of Joseph, God had already worked things out despite the actions of others or the deceiver. God has known the storyline from the start, and He has always had you and I in mind.

My story, as well as yours, is linked together with words like *love, grace, and mercy*!

Joseph the dreamer made it through hard times with incredible character. He had a Hero who, in advance, worked out the details of a plan of freedom for him and his household, that would later save a nation. His story gives us hope that not everything is as it seems. Dreams lived out through destiny have a way of defying the odds to bring us into the garden.

CHARACTER KEY

1. What dreams were you given when you were young?

2. Read Genesis 29. What kind of man was Jacob? Describe the character traits he displayed as he pursued Rachel.

3. In what ways can you identify with Joseph?

4. What was the covenant made with Abraham and what does that mean for you?

5. What dreams have impacted you the most?

6. What kind of character traits do you find admirable in Joseph?

3

THE DAUGHTER'S HERO

He who walks with wise men will be wise, but the companion of fools will suffer harm.

Proverbs 13:20

Once upon a time, there lived a little girl who loved to sing and dance. Braided into the presence of her Creator, creativity flowed in waves of color as she moved in freedom to dance. She loved to twirl around like a ballerina in movements that came without any judgement of herself.

Having the right dress was important. If she had the right dress, she could twirl in circles and feel like the princess she was created to be. If she wore the wrong dress, the dance just wouldn't work. At first, she danced on her own without ever thinking she needed to have someone to dance with. As time went on she began to learn that having the right dance partner was an important part of the story.

This little girl was *me*, and God had fashioned His dream of destiny into my life; the life of a little girl who would dance. From birth, and even as far back as being formed in the womb, destiny is fashioned into every part - body, spirit and soul. Not one of these is separate from the other. Little Mary Lennox's destiny came alive as she searched for the key to the garden door. In spite of experiencing harm from his older brothers who may have been his heroes at one time, Joseph moved into his destiny as he acknowledged his Creator in the midst of his captivity.

Destiny was woven into the pages of that mysterious book with the gold pages that I pulled off the shelf as a little girl and destiny was woven into the fabric of your making and childhood as well.

My first Bible, a storybook of pictures, was received when I was about seven years old. From that book I learned about Jesus and John the Baptist, gathering details mostly from the pictures. I knew there was a God, that somehow Jesus was His Son, and they were both important to me.

There wasn't much talk about the Holy Spirit, and therefore very little was understood. I went to Sunday School in a Lutheran Church and was encouraged from a young age to memorize scripture, which I am grateful for to this day.

Also at the age of seven, I received my first journal. Writing would become a habit cultivated from that time. On the first few pages I wrote about my love for God and my family. A few pages later, I drew hearts around the names of certain boys. It's clear I wanted both my mom and dad to write in the blue and pink pages because their handwriting marked the pages with approval and love.

My first complete Bible containing all of the books in print was received at the start of confirmation class when I was 13. By that time, I had already been kissed by a boy. My young eyes and heart had already been violated. Even so, roots grew down deep from the words and stories I read about in that Bible.

In the midst of learning to talk to God, to pray and to memorize and write scriptures, I referred to the Bible as the "greatest literary treasure in the world" in my journal. I had learned this statement somewhere which gave an acknowledgment to the power of the words that were written.

My mother gave me the gifts of a love for books as well as the value of education. Gifts for special occasions often came in the form of piano and dance lessons, travel with the purpose of education, and books. Playing the piano, writing in my journal, and taking dance and art classes were all activities that caused me to come alive.

I took piano lessons for many years, and eventually competed in the National Guild Auditions. To compete I had to learn four compositions, then play the solo pieces from memory in front of a judge. No one else was allowed in the room but the judge, not even the teacher I had learned from. Each year I would take home a small pin shaped like a piano as an award.

What stayed with me, no matter what happened, was the discipline it took to learn those musical compositions so I could play them later by heart. Many music teachers have used the following quote from *The Pupil's Report Card for the National Piano Guild Auditions* to encourage their students:

> "You have learned the discipline and concentration
> necessary to achieve goals. You have learned how to focus
> and share your talent with adjudicators. You have learned to
> accept both praise as well as constructive criticism with
> poise. In essence, you have learned qualities that will be
> part of your character your entire life."

If there are artists, may they excel in the arts! If there are musically talented daughters, may they sing and play instruments!

It really isn't any wonder I struggled greatly in school when it came to certain math or science subjects. In spite of eventually skipping the classes I seemed to always struggle in, I received A's when it came to anything creative, like writing or the arts. When given something to write or paint my spirit would come alive.

My dad gave me the gift of a strong work ethic. He provided for all of us, working almost everyday of his life just as he saw his dad do. He ran a successful family business that had been passed on from his dad, whom I unfortunately never had the privilege of meeting.

While he was a businessman, my dad also gave me the gift of creativity. His creativity is shown in the home he built, the gardens he has tended too and the works of art he builds for his grandson, my sister's son.

As a family, we created and held to traditions during the holidays. Attending plays like *Joseph and the Amazing Technicolor Dream Coat* and the *Nutcracker* were treasured times spent together enjoying the arts. I have always admired these aspects of my parents, but they were not the only ones who would be a part of shaping my world.

The Heroes of Youth

The period from adolescence through young adulthood is often one of great promise as well as vulnerability. What a girl sees and hears, as well as who she knows, will all play a part in shaping her identity. Her actions are influenced by the world that surrounds her.

Some of what I learned came from the movies and magazines. The characters I saw in the movies weren't necessarily heroes but in my young mind they had what I wanted, which was to create or dance, but also, to be loved and beautiful.

According to the *American Heritage Dictionary*, a hero is described as follows:

1. A person noted for feats of courage or nobility of purpose, especially one who has risked or sacrificed his or her life: soldiers and nurses who were heroes in an unpopular war.

2. A person noted for special achievement in a particular field. [2]

There are heroes and then there are *superheroes*. Most superheroes are made when ordinary people have heroic moments, then the superhero makes a living out of doing good things and accomplishing heroics with certain powers. These characters possess supernatural or superhuman powers and are dedicated to fighting crime, protecting the public and usually battling villains.

Little boys and girls typically have someone they look up to, whether it be a character in movie, a video game or even a book. And of course it is those around them who help shape their character as well.

Men, when they were little boys, may have wanted to be superheroes, build giant forts and rescue the damsel in distress. There is a natural instinct in boys to defeat the enemy and win the war in the games that they play. Little boys have superheroes who show them the kind of man they can be someday.

My husband tells me that as a boy his favorite games were playing in the creek on the farm and building forts. He looked up to his dad who was also a brickmason by trade. The trade would be passed along from generation to generation as was fitting for men who liked to build. As children, he and his brothers built forts and once they finished, they would build another. To this day, my husband loves to build and create. Always wanting to use his hands to be creative, he did not waste time playing video games to try and learn what was expected of him.

As children, some girls have a tendency to create, color, dance, sing and play. They may want to play dress up and dream about prince charming. As I mentioned in the first chapter, my sister and I built forts and that inward desire later showed itself in pink castles, barbie homes and future mansions that offered false safety.

My favorite superhero figure as a young girl was She-Ra. She-Ra had a sword, long beautiful hair, a pink castle in the clouds and an amazing figure, something my Barbie dolls taught me was important from the start. She-Ra's castle was filled with all the right features and furnishings including a princess bed and an elevator that took her from one level to the next.

My favorite movies usually depicted a beautiful girl who was eventually carried away by a handsome prince. The prince always had an array of special skills, was especially protective, and most of all showed the girl a lot of love and flattery. Romeo and Juliet was the ultimate love story in my young mind.

Cinderella was the princess who had my all-time favorite dress. Her dazzling, beautiful blue dress was one of the most iconic dresses in the history of princesses. There was something attractive about the color blue.

One of my favorite memories of my mother and I was when she took me to a fancy department store to find the perfect dress. I tried on gown after gown, feeling like a princess the entire time. Some of the dresses were entirely too expensive to actually consider purchasing, but none-the-less, trying them on and twirling in circles made my heart sing. I eventually settled on a blue dress, the least expensive, but most beautiful to me. Maybe I was reminded of Cinderella who had said, "They can't order me to stop dreaming."

For many of us, the heroes we had in our childhood and those we simply looked up to all played a major role in our thoughts about the world, our identity and our understanding of what was acceptable or not. Whether we believe it or not, what we learned from them taught us about boundaries.

Usually my favorite stories from the books and movies would highlight aspects of desired character traits, but somehow, over time, and with gradual persuasion, some of the characters in the movies or the images on paper brought a violation without any understanding. Whether I wanted them to or not, those characters began to shape my thoughts.

What About Love

Time changed, and I began to admire those who I saw as beautiful. Something shifted and my attention went from looking to someone with the character traits that I thought were important to admiring the people who seemed glamorous. Magazines like

Glamour and *Seventeen* began to influence my thoughts about what was important.

While the movies I continued to watch still portrayed the fairy-tale storyline of a beautiful woman being rescued and romanced, the story would always just come to an end. In all reality, I longed to be rescued.

Often the main character in these movies was taken out of a difficult circumstance where she was being treated poorly or growing up in tough conditions. Cinderella, for example, was forced by her stepmother and stepsisters to do all the house work. In spite of that unfair treatment, Cinderella would always sing and care for her little friends, and that is what I loved most about her character.

Singing was a key for Cinderella.

In my heart, I desired the same things these princesses had. I wanted to be rescued, loved and cherished. The castle sounded like a great place to live with prince charming. Like most young girls, I wondered when I would meet my prince charming.

As I got a little older it was movies like *Dirty Dancing* that would capture my attention. In the film the young character named Baby attracted a good looking, older man. Johnny was the sought-after dance instructor who was teaching at the resort where Baby and her family were spending the summer. Even though Baby's father forbade the relationship, Johnny came back for her in the end. In my young mind it was a perfect love story.

The story showed that Baby and her family only stayed at the summer resort for a few short weeks, and she quickly fell in love with Johnny. Within those few weeks she is seen in bed with her newly met prince, creating the idea for women watching the movie that a heart-throb crush meant love, and love led to sex quite quickly.

Baby taught us that all it took was a little make up, some sexy dance moves and skimpier clothes to snag the man of her dreams. With the purest of motives, my grandma would always fast-forward through the naughty dancing scenes. She believed that seeing people dance provocatively would teach my young female mind that type of behavior was an acceptable way to act and so, those scenes would always be skipped. Of course, I was curious to know what was being avoided, so I eventually found out on my own.

Watching those dance moves made me blush. Strangely, I felt the need to look away, yet something seemed to be drawing me in to pay even more attention.

Dirty Dancing was one of the first major movies that had a subplot of abortion. Even though I watched the movie several times, I didn't really understand what happened in that scene until later in life. A baby was referenced to as a problem that needed to be taken care of.

This movie taught me that my dreams to dance, meet the prince and fall in love somehow meant letting the boundary lines of my garden be crossed. As a little girl, this wasn't what I had been taught, but as I grew older it was easier to make what were seemingly small decisions of compromise. Looking back, I now know that those compromises lined up with what I had seen in the movies and magazines.

What I didn't realize back then was, "For our struggle is not against flesh and blood, but against the rulers, against the powers, against the world forces of this darkness, against the spiritual forces of wickedness in the heavenly places" (Ephesians 6:12). Like thistles and thorns can overtake and eventually destroy the life of a rose, forces of evil were working to overtake and destroy me.

In spite of the forces of evil and even in the midst of thistles and thorns that began to move in, there were roots that grew even deeper than the lies a culture was teaching.

The Strength of a Rose

The remarkable thing about roses is that they can survive for extremely long periods of time. If roses are tended to properly, thistles will not easily grow. If thistles grow, they can always be cut away and destroyed by the gardener.

There is a large rosebush that has covered the wall of the Cathedral of Hildesheim in Germany for over 1000 years. Believed to be the oldest living rose in the world, this rosebush is proof of the strength of a rose.

During the fifteenth century, factions fighting to control England used the rose as a symbol. The white rose represented York, and the red rose, Lancaster. The conflict between them became known as the "War of the Roses."

No matter the weather, a rose can survive because of roots that go down deep to provide nourishment. That nourishment not only comes from nutrients in the soil, but also from light and water. Roses find nourishment with their deep root systems which allow them to receive strength and empowerment from places of life.

While, like the rose, I found nourishment in deep places where my spirit came alive, there were thistles tugging me in other directions. It felt as if those thistles were robbing me of creativity and hope. Often, when thorns and thistles show up in our lives, we stop doing the things we once loved.

While my heart may have kept beating through the war, the thorns cut deeply. As my heroes changed over time, so too did my actions.

INFLUENCE KEY

1. What were some of the seeds of truth that were planted in your life when you were young? For example: do you remember any Bible stories or scriptures?

2. Who was your favorite hero and why? What kind of characteristics did your favorite hero have?

3. Were there any movies, magazines or people that you believe poisoned your thinking?

4. Was there someone who you looked up to in your childhood and, if so, why?

5. Name the three closest people in your life and write about the character traits you admire in each of them.

4

THISTLES AND THORNS OF VIOLATION

Two things cannot be in one place. Where you tend a rose, my lad, a thistle cannot grow.

Frances Hodgson Burnett

Like Joseph, I too was sold for a price. I became stuck in the thorns of deceit. Although there were some delightful memories as a young girl, life would soon change and good memories would fade. Clouds blocked the sunlight, keeping me from growing towards what was good.

Violation came first in the forms of pictures on paper that shaped my idea of sexuality. The moments leading up to other violations and exchange of self were gradual in compromise. Like many of us, when I was young I was vulnerable and easily swayed. A few factors may have increased my personal level of vulnerability, but none-the-less, these moments of deceit came like thistles. A thistle is just another word for dishonor and violation.

When we value something or someone, honor is shown through our words and actions. Had I been able to see the value in who I was, as well as who others were, some of the violating moments may not have occurred. Other moments of violation were brought on by the actions of others. Those violations were like thorns to destroy and some of those moments caught me by complete surprise.

A thistle is the name of a plant characterized by leaves with sharp prickles. In scripture, plants of this class were a symbol of desolation. In Proverbs 24:31 we are told, "And behold, it was completely overgrown with thistles; its surface was covered with nettles, and its stone wall was broken down." This proverb is speaking about a neglected field or vineyard, which very well could have been within garden walls.

While thistles may actually have some known therapeutic effects, in essence, they are invasive and destructive. Sharp prickles cut and tear at roses that would rather drink water and grow towards the light with the right kind of love.

In the Book of Hosea, thorns serve to block the path of the one who is going after pleasures and chasing after other lovers. Out of love, it is God who blocks Gomer's actions with thorns as she goes after what is not good for her:

> And she will seek them, but will not find them. Then she will say, "I will go back to my first husband, for it was better for me then than now." (Hosea 2:7)

This scripture is talking about Gomer, who was the wife of the Prophet Hosea. Gomer's unfaithfulness and Hosea's forgiveness symbolized God's forgiving love for unfaithful Israel and His unfaithful Bride who goes after other lovers. Other lovers could be the love of money, fame, drugs or alcohol, or in Gomer's case, men other than her husband.

With decisions or violations that cross boundaries, thistles prevent the way forward. When compromising choices or unintentional violations brought on by others are kept hidden and not talked about, thistles will grow.

Poison as Thistles on Pages

The boys must have found the magazine somewhere. They weren't very careful about keeping it hidden. Having been ripped from the seam of the magazine, pages were scattered about. The pages could have flown in on the wind from across town. Or, maybe they came from somewhere nearby. It didn't matter.

The wind carried page after page of violation and placed it in our picturesque front yard. We lived in a middle class neighborhood where all the homes were really quite beautiful. They weren't cookie-cutter houses, but each uniquely designed for the family that would make their home inside its brick walls. Clutter and litter certainly had no place on our property, and especially not the pages that had blown in.

With childhood curiosity, I innocently flipped over the first page. Like a thorn brings violation, my mind was instantly pierced. I was young, maybe nine or ten years old, and had just returned home from a piano lesson. The vile images that covered that glossy paper were never meant for my young eyes to see.

That was the very first moment I unintentionally learned about sex.

My young eyes, untainted by the poison of lust until that moment, momentarily gazed at the picture of two women and two men. Each person in the photo was positioned to touch another near places that were meant to be private and not exposed. So many boundaries were crossed. Somewhere in my young heart I knew this was not right and that I was not supposed to be seeing anything like what I was looking at. In that moment, the vulgar images were strongly imprinted on my mind and the violation could not be undone.

I do not recall exactly what I did with those pages. Surely I either tossed them back into the wind or threw them away. I wish I could say that each page was burned - the ashes scattered into the wind to be carried off just as easily as the pages had blown in.

The magazine pages were from *Hustler*, a pornographic magazine published by Larry Flynt. So clearly, as evidenced by the portrayal of what I saw, the content he published was the most sexually explicit and controversial available at that time. As a result, Flynt was called before the Supreme Court of the United States on three separate occasions. The verdicts were issued in his favor, however, I am saying to you:

> *Watch, watch and see, the people versus Flynt has been reversed in the Courts of Heaven. A verdict has been issued and all that has come forth in the form of print to violate so many young minds is coming to an end. Watch, watch and see, as this empire built on greed, lust and perversion falls. Fire burns up what is vile.*

Another thistle was the secrecy of what I had seen. My voice would not be heard speaking up about this violation because I did not know who I could tell or how I would tell them. No one asked about or brought up such things.

Silence became betrayal to self.

My young mind did not know how to communicate about such poison, yet the images were far too easy to be stumbled upon.

Around the same age of that violation, my friend and I would get together to play with our Barbie dolls, all of the best of course. I loved dressing the dolls in brightly colored clothes. My Barbie had everything she was supposed to. She had all the right clothes, the perfect body and the pink Caddy to go with her style. She also had Ken, the cutest out of all the guy dolls.

We were caught up in the midst of playing in our Barbie City built in pink one day when my friend said she wanted to show me something. Her parents were not home and she informed me of how important it was that what she was about to do be kept between us. Following her into her dad's bedroom, I watched as she pulled out a stack of magazines that had been shoved way under the bed, apparently to be kept out of sight.

I was probably 11 or 12 years old when I saw those violating images that shaped my idea of sexuality. While I hated what I saw, it stirred something in me that I didn't understand.

The first time a boy had kissed me I was very young, maybe Kindergarten. While it was just a kiss on the cheek, I liked the way it made me feel, like I was special to receive such attention. I later wrote about my first real kiss at the age of 12, that he was my whole world and surely the one I would marry.

What I had lacked at a young age was the understanding of boundaries and a healthy sexuality. I had learned about such in the wrong ways. This dialogue of healthy sexuality needs to start at an early age. These conversations would be most effective when presented in relationship to the scriptures. The Lord is saying:

> *No longer will my Bride be silent. The time is here when sexuality will be talked about in the church, from a biblical standpoint, in safe places and with safe people who understand the significance of this topic. Analogies will be given to teach the significance of boundaries. Young boys will seek to show honor by not crossing boundaries and young girls will act in ways that demonstrate they know their worth and will be treated with honor. They will demonstrate they know their worth by their actions.*

Thistles and Thorns

Although strong roots of truth had grown deep in my young heart, vulnerabilities were displayed like fragile rose petals. It was the progression of gradual, curious choices that I made from a vulnerable heart, as well as the violations brought on by others that pierced my soul.

Scripture verses lined the pages of some of my earliest journals, but they were mixed with words about the latest heart-throb obsession that had captured my attention. These conflicting emotions of youth were dramatic.

In a student journal, likely from the period of time surrounding my confirmation classes, I once wrote about God. The story of Job was a fascination of mine. I felt like I could identify with the emotions that he experienced. While I had love for God and believed in Jesus Christ, I was tempted to take a path laden with thistles. I did not know how to protect the boundary lines of my garden.

Many times my boundary lines were crossed without my permission, including the first time a boy showed me pornography on a video tape. I would not have chosen to learn about sexuality again in that way. The magazine pages that had brought an intrusion through the gates of my eyes made the way for this video to bring poison into my soul.

Even in the midst of reading and studying the Word of God and having a type of prayer life, I became entangled in a culture that was seeped in drugs, dishonor and music that seemed to be paired with pills the color of candy. Forms of dishonor of any kind are traumatic for a young mind. At that young age, I longed for acceptance and using drugs and alcohol quickly became an illusion of such. Addiction was a swiftly formed byproduct of use that came with dishonor.

The effects of alcoholism in the home created a constant crises in the form of screaming, slammed doors and distant relationships with little communication. I was in a war zone of addiction and teenage emotions. Faced with the inability to know how to handle those emotions I was experiencing, and likely influenced by something dark, I would retreat to my room to take my mind off the battle. I wanted to feel something else, something other than the never-ending, raw emotions.

I was in the midst of heartache when I was sent off to the first facility. My young heart felt broken as I tried to navigate my way through what I thought was love. What I didn't understand at that time is that when I had sex for the first time, I was coming together with him - body, spirit and soul. I couldn't really understand the depths of this connection nor the effects of the drugs and alcohol on my teenage self. My spirit and soul, and the emotions I felt, could not let go. Love was awakened before its time.

> I adjure you, O daughters of Jerusalem, by the gazelles or by the does of the field, that you not stir up or awaken love until it pleases. (Song of Solomon 2:7)

My emotions and thoughts were like raging winds. Having received a prescription for Paxil, things got worse. I later discovered in my college years that Paxil was one of the medications on the list named "Pandora's Box." Some of the medications on that list were found to cause suicidal thoughts. It was at that time that doctors were instructed not to prescribe Paxil to anyone under the age of 18. The so-called solution to all my problems, the pill prescribed to me at 14 years old, had caused severe thoughts that led to attempted suicide. Death was given to me in the form of a pill prescribed by a doctor.

Not knowing what to do with me, and doing what they thought was best, my parents sent me away again. First, I was brought to a hospital with a psychiatric unit, but after becoming involved with drugs and alcohol, I was sent to treatment centers.

When I came home from my first treatment center at 14, I was greeted by a friend who welcomed me back with the invitation to get high. My journey of being influenced and affected by toxins continued for the next ten years. The thorns and thistles of drug and alcohol use affected everything.

Shame built up over the years. I wrestled with wanting to stay close to God, but felt like I was growing further a part from Him. There was a war raging on the inside and the drugs took my mind off that war, creating within me a new experience that I would often retreat to. Boyfriends were always present. Drugs were always available. Eventually, my focus towards what I once loved faded and I quit playing piano, painting and being creative.

I moved out of my parent's the moment I turned 18 - in fact, I may have even been 17. This was a year that so many things changed. Leaving the nest was liberating as it gave me more freedom and privacy. I was tired of the constant influence of alcoholism in the home, a thistle growing in my life in more than one way. In the midst of drug and alcohol addiction also came other addictions and the greatest heartache I would ever know.

Dark Angel

June 27, 2001 was the day that would forever change everything in my life, and I mean everything. I had just turned 18, but it was at 17 that deceit would come to cut out life. I withered away in a deep darkness of secrecy, shame and silence. Developing thorns of my own after this great violation, I sought to keep away from anything or anyone that tried to get close. Piercing my spirit and soul, the thistles grew deep by wrapping and twisting themselves around me.

The boundary lines between what was right and what was wrong, good and evil, life and death, had been crossed. Silence, drowning in grief, shut the door to the garden. My path was completely blocked. My song would appear to have been stolen. Those days, I dressed as a dark angel at the rave parties I began to frequent. My soul and spirit mimicked what had caused death on that dismal day.

After what I had experienced, nothing else could ever be as black.

He Found Me

Still in high school, but fading from the lifestyle of a teenager who once played piano, painted, danced as a ballerina, and wrote, my attention was drawn towards what brought momentary relief but ultimately left a feeling of misery. Using drugs at a young age quickly brought a thrill and a facade of acceptance. Instead of playing piano, which had always been enjoyable, drugs provided a rush. I gradually stopped pursuing the experience playing music had once provided.

Other than a few get-togethers at 11 or 12 where strip poker became a part of the weekend, I hadn't been asked to remove my clothes. It wasn't until I was 17 that I was asked by my boyfriend if I would dance for his friends at a small gathering. I didn't quite understand his question, but with persuasion he gave instructions about the actions that were expected. Somewhere in a drug induced state, I justified acting out the strip tease. Perhaps this was for approval.

His persistence paid off.

He made me feel *desirable*, something I wanted to feel.

It was the friend I was asked to dance for who further pursued me. What I didn't understand at that time, is that I had been handled like something to be given. I couldn't help but wonder if this had been pre-arranged. This was the grooming process.

This new man was much older and he showed much more affection. We spent much of our time together in a home where drug trafficking was prevalent. This was a place where large amounts of cash were being handled. People came and went just as often as gatherings centered around use would occur.

At the time, I was still trying to finish high school. I knew education was important, so I enrolled at a local alternative school while working a part time job to pay for my apartment.

My new older "boyfriend" began to do things that showed he cared. He showed affection, bought gifts and brought excitement into my life. He was dealing large amounts of substances, so drug use was typically a part of our times together.

He was the one who introduced me to the industry.

Walking into that building for the first time brought excitement. I felt a thrill deep inside that danced on a thin line of excitement, glamor and seduction. There I was, in a strip club with the man who had stolen my heart. It didn't matter that he was much older. He made me feel adored.

When he brought me into that club for the first time it really wasn't difficult at all for me to fit in. I had already taken my clothes off at 17, under the influence of substances and at the invitation of performing a "harmless strip tease."

The manager of the club came over to our table as soon as we sat down. With a tone of curiosity and excitement, he asked if I wanted to take a tour of the massive three-story building. He told me I would make a lot of money as he looked me up and down, grinning with approval. I was quickly convinced there was something there for me.

Around that same time, my boyfriend had been taking me to other clubs in the area. When we returned to the first club we had visited, it was easier to say yes to that manager's suggestions.

Had this set up been pre-arranged?

Had I been targeted in some way?

Whether visible or invisible, entanglements were set up for my entrance into the industry. The life was a fit that resembled the culture that I had been brought into.

So began the years of lights, a painted face and a heart closed off. I was in the life that was deemed as entertainment. The lights were bright, the music was loud and the life seemed glamorous for a time. While working at the club I managed to enroll in college, but that endeavor did not last long.

Like Joseph in the Old Testament, violations brought me into Egypt. My heart, like a door to a garden filled with life, had already been shut. Nothing else could really bring the kind of black that June had brought. I danced and gave myself away, while immersed in money, seduction, drugs and alcohol.

It was not a dream as a little girl to grow up and one day dance in a strip club. This was not the kind of dance taught in my childhood classes. Dreams of singing, writing, dancing and creating were slowly dying. Choices that caused me to feel alive were gradually taken over by thistles.

The boundary lines faded and I became enmeshed in a culture of intoxication.

BOUNDARIES KEY

1. Were there any kind of violations that crossed your boundaries when you were young?

2. How did you first learn about sex and/or sexuality? Would you say this was a healthy way to learn?

3. Has something ever happened to you that you felt you couldn't talk about? Is there someone who you could tell now?

4. As a teenager or young adult, was there ever someone who captured your attention? Write about this, and/or your first heart-throb and first heartache.

5. What boundaries do you feel were crossed in your teenage years?

5

A RUBY'S WORTH

She is more precious than rubies; nothing you desire can compare with her.

Proverbs 3:15

"Mya, $450! Angel, $375! Shannon, $400!" Reading off the totals one-by-one from his clipboard, the manager loudly called out each of our stage names. A fake name, followed by a number. The managers who were on shift always sat in the same place at the end of the night. Nothing ever changed, except the girls who came in and out of the club.

My stage name, Shannon, was a fake name to go with the fake identity that had been molded by some facet of culture that told me I was more desirable if I acted, dressed and painted my face in a certain way. My worth was based on a number and the attention or number of dances I acquired each night. Somewhere along the lines, I had believed the lie that my value was found in what I looked like, the shape of my body, and what I could do that brought pleasure. The more money I made, the higher my value, or so I thought.

In order to keep track of each couch and bed dance, the floor managers carried around clipboards all night. Hearing my stage name followed by a number meant I could come forward and pay the house a percentage of what I had earned that night. Sometimes my worth was high, sometimes it was low. Every couch dance, bed dance and VIP bed dance was tallied up, so the managers knew just about how much was earned and just how much was expected to be paid.

I would wait to hear the tally and wonder if I had a high number that night or if I would feel the embarrassment of a low number being called out in front of all the other girls and managers.

Based on how my night went, there was an understanding of whether I would hear a high or low number to be paid in. If more was made, it meant plenty of regulars had come in to pay for my time.

What was I worth that night?

Numbers would not be called out until each girl came down from the dressing room. Once we were all downstairs the managers would call aloud the totals owed. Everybody knew that the more you made, the more you would pay in. If you didn't pay in as much, you hadn't made much. This entire moment was humiliating for so many reasons which made it one of my motivators for trying to leave early.

Trying to make an early exit was met with the managers saying, "Pay up," or "No, you can't leave, it's only 2 a.m." Yes, I had signed a contract, but handing close to half my earnings over was never any less vexing. Nevertheless, I kept dancing and they kept earning. I also learned the hard way that if I didn't tip the bouncers, I would receive less protection from customers. If I didn't tip the DJ, he wouldn't play the songs I wanted when I went on stage.

The whole system was all based on manipulation and coercion fueled by greed. Another place I saw manipulation, coercion and greed was at the party mansion I was brought to. It was a second or third home of one of the club's owners. This was a place where many of the girls I worked with were brought to for parties. It was at this mansion where I realized I wasn't the only girl one of the managers was going after.

Even so, I could not get away from the ever-increasing advances of this one manager in particular. If I tried to leave before 2 a.m., I faced his advancements in the coat closet near the exit door. The small room was the perfect cramped space to count the cash, hand in the cash, and fight off advancements.

In that small room, I was faced with the choice to either cave in or force a smile and say something witty to get out of that small space. And yet, there was something in me that liked the attention from an older man. Somehow, in an unhealthy way, I felt desirable.

It always took time to change, gather my things off the large vanity in the dressing room and come downstairs to the main floor. The 3rd floor was for the VIP area, which contained beds separated by thin coverings to give an illusion of privacy. Also on the 3rd floor, there was the large dressing room filled with lockers, a vanity counter top, and mirrors. My locker, number 32, housed the contents of a young woman who was far from living out her dream.

Gathering my things meant collecting make-up and a designer bag that usually held a hidden stash of some kind. The drugs were easy to come by; I either purchased my high from one of the girls or one of my regulars would provide the supply.

My go-to drugs in those days were cocaine and especially ecstasy. The toxic love affair that I had with MDMA had started at only 17 and quickly progressed in the midst of the night life and especially, my work place.

By the time I came down the three flights of stairs or riding the elevator to the bottom floor at the end of the night, my high would gradually be fading. Occasionally, if I had taken the drug later in the evening, or if I had taken more than the normal dose, the effect would still be experienced, which meant I had to navigate my way back to my apartment in the bright lights of the city night. As time progressed, leaving the club meant leaving with some of the girls I considered friends. It was better for us to use together than alone.

When life circumstances, choices and coercion from others create entanglements, the pressure creates change. Gems, for example, change under pressure. Although I was being formed under pressure, it would take several more years before the pressure produced healthy change. There comes a point at which a person knows something different has to happen.

In this way, precious gems are similar to God's precious daughters. Gems symbolize beauty and value, and, just like people, gems can form under pressure.

Gems Under Pressure

Gems, or precious stones, can be cut from ordinary rocks like clay, copper, iron, or coal. A rock has a 1/282 chance to produce a gem when mining. It is even possible to mine multiple gems from the same rock.

Rubies are one of the most popular gems for good reasons. Fine quality rubies are some of the most expensive gems, with record prices of over $100,000 per carat. The beautiful, red-colored gem is exceptionally durable and one of the few precious stones whose color reaches vivid saturation levels. The color red also reminds us of the precious blood that Jesus shed.

Another reason for their popularity is that rubies are subjected to more treatments than almost any other gem. After diamonds, rubies are the second hardest natural mineral, making them exceptionally durable. One of the most remarkable things about the formation of rubies is that geologists are not sure how formation happens. The very existence of rubies is something of a minor geological miracle.

This unique set of circumstances makes rubies rare.

A commonly held belief among geologists is that rubies are formed by tectonic plates smashing together, as the India and Asia plates did when the Himalayas were formed, forcing limestone deposits deep into the earth where intense heat and pressure caused sparkly marble.

In Proverbs 3:15, we read, "She is more precious than jewels; And nothing you desire compares with her." In this divinely inspired writing, Solomon was referring to wisdom. We are encouraged to seek wisdom from the One who created us as if we were searching for a fine jewel. Then, during a time of pressure, the gem is formed by taking action according to that wisdom. Clearly, gems go though refining in times of pressure.

Famously, the writer of Proverbs 31 describes a virtuous wife as being "worth far more than rubies." The word *virtuous* means "moral, ethical and honest."

In Isaiah 54, a life chapter for me, an eternal covenant of peace speaks of the heritage of the servants of the Lord. Isaiah tells us that rubies were placed within the boundary walls and jewels were set upon the gates of what is portrayed as garden walls. The verse symbolizes the boundary walls of life and reveals the future when Zion's walls will be covered in precious stones. It is God who will, "make your battlements of rubies, and your gates of crystal, and your entire wall of precious stones" (Isaiah 54:12).

One of my favorite scriptures about jewels can be found in Zechariah where the prophet speaks towards the coming Messiah: "The Lord their God will save His people on that day as a shepherd saves his flock. They will sparkle in His land like jewels in a crown" (Zechariah 9:16 NIV).

While this chapter was being written, the Lord gave me a picture of a beautiful garden wall covered in rubies. I hear the Lord saying to His daughters:

My Dearest Daughter, You are more valuable to me than many jewels. You are my chosen one, more precious than rubies. Allow me to be a safe place and let us together draw the boundary lines of this garden in pleasant places, for indeed, dearest one, you have a beautiful inheritance.

Walls create boundaries and rubies are exceptionally durable and brilliant in color. My garden wall needed the virtuous rubies of character that would set boundaries to live empowered by God's wisdom.

Fueling the Industry

Boundaries get crossed in a life of seduction, lust and greed.

Pharaoh profited from the work of the Israelites, even though the Israelites were God's people. In the same way, the owners and mangers of the strip club all received profit. Their profits came from me uncovering myself and providing my body as contact during lap or bed dances. My job was to arouse and bring excitement to those who would pay. I had become a commodity, just a body. That is just how the industry works.

I profited financial gain from the exposure of my body at the sake of losing my soul, my song and the dreams that I had when I was a little girl. I was totally and completely submerged in the realities of the industry. Those of us who have lived the story are the ones who must speak the story in His perfect timing, for this is how we overcome.

> And they overcame him because of the blood of the Lamb and because of the word of their testimony, and they did not love their life even when faced with death. (Revelation 12:11)

Many times I convinced myself that I needed the money, or that it really wasn't that bad. The reality was that the cycle never ended and the entanglements kept me coming back.

There were times in the beginning when I thought the lifestyle was glamorous. The thing about slavery is that it subtly woos you with its entrapments. There is a difference between darkness and light, and what is actually dark may appear to be illuminated as a false light. When something seeped in evil appears good, the reality of the deception weighs on the spirit, body and soul.

An industry of exploitation and manipulation and the *sales* of daughters is an industry where dishonor breeds. Where dishonor breeds, so does secrecy and grief.

Where strip clubs are permitted, exploitation exists. Where exploitation is permitted, the trafficking of drugs and people also exist.

Although treated like and acting as such, I was never meant to be a commodity - my body separate from my spirit and soul - for those who would exchange money for a momentary body pleasure that brought sexual arousal. As the routine wore on, deep down inside, I began to hate what I was doing.

There were sporadic moments when I cleared out my locker and told the girls all my clothes were for sale. Typically, if something more dramatic than what I found acceptable happened at the club, I declared my intent to quit and tried walking out. Sometimes I just gave away my prized garments of seduction as I stormed out of the club, only to be confronted by the manager on the main floor.

The cycle continued.

There was always one more bill to pay or one more empty promise to myself that I would only stay a little while longer. No matter the war I was experiencing, the men kept coming into the club. They kept spending money and I kept taking it like a well-groomed body commodity.

Time and Chance Can Break You

Sometimes I forgot how tormented I felt during this time. I suppose I would have grasped at anything that offered comfort. He found me because he was looking for someone to break.

I was already broken.

When he came into the club, he made it a point to get my attention. I could feel his gaze and it felt good. I liked the feelings that were stirred up by knowing his attention was solely on me. Gracing his table, the place where he always sat, I played the part of seductive Shannon.

The enemy whispered, "Play the part, just play the part."

A routine was developed with him in mind that I played out well. Spending a little time with him at the table was for the purpose of enticing him. Eventually he would ask for a dance, but he always chose the less expensive couch dances. He never spent much money, because he was just playing the game. His consistent and continued efforts at coming into the club made it easy for me to accept his invitation to go out to dinner. I took a chance on him, thinking he was good looking and rationalizing that he must have cared about me since he came to see me so often.

For the first few months he was sweet. He took me out to fancy places around the city. After a while, I started going to his home after work so we could spend more time together. He had coke whenever I wanted it, and drinking was typically a part of our time together.

Something changed after several months. He began to show his temper, displaying some kind of ownership over me. When he came into the club he wasn't the same as he used to be. Instead, he closely watched my every move. Fueled by drug and alcohol use, fights erupted between us.

He eventually asked what I thought about an escort service, something I didn't have much understanding of. I balked at the suggestion, showing a response that was not well received.

In his home, at the time of this exchange, it was time for me to leave. Without a driver's license, I finally called for a cab, which gave unwanted time to fight. Once the cab showed up, I was chased outside with the accompaniment of rocks hurled in my direction. Nevertheless, I quickly got into the car and screamed at the driver to leave. The rocks continued to hit the cab as we sped off.

The driver looked at me in the rear view mirror with shock in his eyes and asked, "Ma'am are you okay?" All I could do was cry.

When we got to my apartment and I stepped out of the cab, I realized that we had been followed. The cab driver looked at me again, wondering what to do. At this point, it was fight or flight and all I had left in me was flight. I ran to my apartment building which allowed access on the first level. My hope was to get up to my apartment in time to lock the door.

He made his way behind me, up the stairs and to the front door of my apartment. Even though I shut the door, the entanglement that I had with this man gave me little choice other than to open the door. He was screaming and banging on the door, and in my twisted thinking, I thought that if I opened it up he would stop.

He said he wanted the money he knew I had stashed somewhere in my corner apartment. I didn't know any of my neighbors but I have to wonder if they had ever heard anything. Surely they heard him yelling, demanding with physical force that I give him the money that I took home from the club. He said he knew I kept a stash in my apartment and he wasn't going to leave without it. Because I just wanted him to leave, and I was scared, I handed over the money.

I was a lot more willing to hand over the money to the managers in the club, like I was trained to do. Handing over the money to this man was out of fear.

My world had become isolated.

The only people I knew were those at the club and a few people in college who knew nothing of my life. After about two years at the community college I dropped out because I couldn't see the point of continuing. I could hardly get there during the day because of the hours of life in the industry.

When he finally left my apartment that night, I was so frightened that I made a call to the first person I thought could help. After all, there was some kind of strange relationship going on. The club manager I called showed up later that night like a knight in shinning armor. It turned out his armor wasn't so shiny. He was more covered with dishonor that was capable of further violation.

Not long after this, another incident transpired that resulted in my phone being taken. That time I was able to reach out to my mom, who quickly made her way to where I was. Together, we went down to the police department and recovered my phone that law enforcement had obtained from him. Not many questions were asked. A recommendation to meet with a woman's advocate was given, but never followed through with. I never thought of myself as a woman who was being abused. I couldn't see the point of a restraining order because he wouldn't follow it anyway. Besides, I wasn't sure if I wanted to completely push him away.

Didn't I care about him?

Didn't he care about me?

As my mother and I drove away from the police station, I finally got a chance to open my phone. My heart sank as I saw that all the numbers in my phone had been deleted, except for his.

I didn't realize at the time what he was trying to do. It wasn't until eight or nine years into my sobriety that I learned about the tactics of pimps. I see now that my world was layered in exploitation, but that was a word that wasn't in my vocabulary at that time.

The "relationship" did not progress much after that. What happened had scared me enough to get away from him, but not without the aid of the club and manager who I began to see as a place of safety in some twisted way.

Oppressing Puppet Master

My body on a stage, once a little girl with hopes and dreams, for all to see.

An exchange of $1 bills, maybe a $5 or $10 and if I was valued high enough, I received a $20 or $100 for arousal. It wasn't just my body that was being exposed, but my soul as well. Towards the end, somewhere deep inside, I hated what was happening. I became angry and the unresolved grief of my long-kept secret was literally killing me. I wasn't singing anymore and I certainly wasn't dancing how I was intended to. I wasn't creating anything of honor or beauty.

If someone was really seeking to get my attention, they placed a few twenties or some hundred dollar bills on the stage. The more a man set out, the more attention he would get. That's what the industry is all about - the sale of self. If a person had the money, that's where my attention would go. The goal was to make money.

There are certain environments that perpetuate greed and lust and I was in one of them. So was every single person that walked through the door of that club. It was all like a play and those who participated were like puppets held up by strings of entanglements connected to some dark puppet master with an evil motive.

I was once told that those who stay in the club more than five years have a harder time of getting out. It was easy to stay stuck in that life, even though it was getting harder to breathe. Life intersected with exploitation through the porn culture. I received offers to be in the club's magazines and to travel to the owners' other clubs in different states. After traveling to Miami, I ended up in a nightmare induced by too many drugs and too few boundaries.

Stronger than the entanglements to the pharaohs who played their parts was the cry in my heart that was being heard all along. Like a strong root, grace brought connection to the vine of life. I fled to Montana to try to get away from the industry, but when your life is entangled in slavery, no matter where you go, there you are.

GEM KEY

1. What pressures in life have you risen up from or are you now being drawn out of?

2. Have you known someone who was coercive or manipulating? What actions revealed those character traits? In what ways have you shown manipulation?

3. Identify and write scriptures that you find in the Bible that have to do with gems. Share about these scriptures and any revelation (understanding) you receive.

4. Who is the puppet master with an evil motive as mentioned at the end of the chapter? What scriptures can you find about him?

5. What stuck out to you in this chapter and why do you think that is?

6

THE IRON FURNACE

But the Lord has taken you and brought you out of the iron furnace, out of Egypt, to be a people of His own inheritance, as you are this day.

Deuteronomy 4:20

You can only be in an iron furnace for so long. When Egypt and Israel were first introduced to each other Joseph the Israelite occupied a signifiant place of influence in Pharaoh's palace. After the generation of Joseph departed and the Israelites lost their influence, Egypt became their captors instead of their benefactors. Egypt had given the Israelites land, shelter, and produce. They provided anything the Israelites might need. Then, over time, the people were exploited and their residence in Egypt became an *iron furnace* of slavery.

The Israelites, God's chosen people, originally came to Egypt to find relief from a terrible famine, and subsequently they became enslaved. God desired to bring His people out of the harsh rule of Pharaoh.

Slavery works by subtle deception that progresses to cross the boundary lines. I was not deceived overnight, but over a progression of time. I had been groomed into believing my needs were getting met by those who crossed my boundary lines. I did not have a clear understanding of what my boundaries were. The illusion that some of my needs were being met kept me in the furnace. Violation, greed and betrayal were at the core of every aspect of my life and I was crying out on the inside.

> Furthermore I have heard the groaning of the sons of Israel, because the Egyptians are holding them in bondage, and I have remembered My covenant. Say, therefore, to the sons of Israel, 'I am the Lord, and I will bring you out from under the burdens of the Egyptians, and I will deliver you from their bondage. I will also redeem you with an outstretched arm and with great judgments. Then I will take you for My people, and I will be your God; and you shall know that I am the Lord your God, who brought you out from under the burdens of the Egyptians. (Exodus 6:5-7)

Montana Mountains

Moving to Montana for a season seemed like a good escape; however, wherever you go, there you are. If you're stuck in the furnace, changing locations doesn't usually work. The mindset of a slave doesn't change with a change in scenery alone. I wanted to leave the industry, but the industry didn't want to let me go.

In my own strength, I could not quit using. I was a slave to the very substances that had initially provided feelings of pleasure and an escape from the grief that was blackening my soul. For a time, I had fun using. The drug and alcohol use was just a part of the lifestyle, late nights, parties and the fake relationships wrapped in greed. There were no boundaries.

It was as if there was an invisible chain of attachment that kept me bound to the industry. My mind was held captive with the seductive thoughts that would, once ripened, influence my every action. Everyday I faced triggers that influenced my thoughts to go back. Those triggers came disguised as songs, unpaid or upcoming bills or just thoughts of getting high.

There has been this false illusion of exploitation or trafficking meaning someone would be physically locked in a basement room or chained to bed, and although this can happen, it is more prevalent that the "chains" to the exploitive industry are disguised as entanglements. These entanglements may be in the form of drugs, money, the illusion of a relationship, men and women acting as pimps, or managers who use tactics of coercion, fraud and manipulation.

The entanglements can always be traced back to the same root - the *vine of Sodom* as Moses spoke of in Deuteronomy 32:32. "For their vine is from the vine of Sodom, and from the fields of Gomorrah; Their grapes are grapes of poison, Their clusters, bitter." The vine of Sodom has fruit called "Apples of Sodom," which, though beautiful to the eye, are toxic when eaten.

The coercion from the managers, the toxic thinking, the drugs - all of it kept me bound to a repetitive cycle that seemed impossible to break out of.

When you are addicted to drugs and alcohol and know where you can get your fix, along with the money you've been groomed to make, it is much easier to walk through the doors of the furnace, even though it burns.

It was in Montana where I tried to leave Egypt and learn a new way of life. It took a few more attempts, a few more highs, and another broken relationship to truly break out.

The mountains and the beauty of God's country left an imprint of something beautiful on my heart. While there were many good things about Montana, I was still in the furnace. What I knew was how to earn money in a club, so for a short time, I gravitated to a club in the area. I ended up getting kicked out for taking more of a cut than the house mom would allow. That's the way the industry works - it's all about profit. She had been checking on my loyalty and I had none for her.

There was a war raging within. As much as I wanted to hold onto the relationship I was in, I was not able. It was there, in Montana, that I got to know my then boyfriend's family. Because we had established a relationship during that time, his parents were available to counsel me after I moved back to Minnesota and faced yet another crisis.

Thankfully, both his mom and dad were in their own process of recovery. They understood that for those caught in the grips addiction, there are rock bottom moments that can lead to change. During my own rock bottom moment, emerging from a nightmare in Miami, they were the ones who talked me through getting the help that I so desperately needed.

Back in Minnesota

"Save me from the nothing I've become!"

The words sounded through the speakers, over and over.

"Save me from the nothing I've become."

The lyrics sung by Amy Lee of the band Evanescence captured exactly what I was feeling towards the end of my time in the furnace.

The songs played as my cue to enter onto the stage at the club.

One of the last times I was on stage, everything became so real. Prior to this moment I had attempted leaving the club several times, only to end up right back. The culture had become my life and I was trapped in the iron furnace. Each time I attempted to leave, one of the managers would say, "You'll be back."

I hated that they were right. It was so hard to get away.

Every second of that last moment on stage I felt nothing but anger. With no expression on my face, there was no fake smile to crack. As had become my routine, I swirled around the poles, each move a well-rehearsed action that meant absolutely nothing.

"Without a soul, my spirit is sleeping somewhere cold... Wake me up inside... Got to open my eyes to everything, Don't let me die here...Bring me to life!"

The words from the song "Bring me To Life" echoed through the enormous three story club and the words mimicked the sound of my soul. The young man at the tip rail turned towards his friends and laughed, then he looked back at me and thew out another stack of cash. With a loud voice that mimicked the song booming through the club he exclaimed, "I'll save you."

This was my existence. At that moment, I felt so many things I hated. This is what I had been groomed to do. The drugs were the only things that numbed the pain and shame that I had tucked deep down inside. Even those entanglements were not working anymore.

"Call my name and save me from the dark bid my blood to run, before I come undone; Save me from the nothing I've become"

Nearly six years prior to that moment, I was the young girl who was told I would make a lot of money upon my first entrance into that club. I had been deceived into believing the lies that the industry of exploitation told. The truth was, I was only desirable for nothing more than a body pleasure. The reality of this truth and the lies that I believed hit me as this young man threw out his dollars and laughed with his friends.

I felt so broken.

I was strung out that night and when that truth began to hit me I had to escape from reality. My spirit was crying out, "O Lord, from the depths of despair I cry for your help: 'Hear me! Answer! Help me'" (Psalm 130:1 TLB).

Escaping from reality meant taking more drugs, and making money at the club was the way to get the drugs, unless they came from a man. It wasn't just the substances that kept me coming back, but also the invisible entanglements that became like a yoke around my neck. At the club, I had learned to earn to provide for myself what I thought was important. It was also at the club where, strangely, the people became like family - except this family brought violation.

I was too dead inside to even recognize the deep-rooted grief that kept me from the garden. Unseen shackles kept me attached to the things that were slowly destroying me. Severe drug and alcohol addiction, faulty thinking, low self-worth, obsession over money and the constant coercion from one of the managers kept me entangled.

Simply deciding to quit working at the club and get a normal job would not be easy. After being hooked on making fast money and using drugs to escape reality, just getting a normal eight-to-five job doesn't suddenly make life all better.

I tried leaving many times.

One attempt in particular came after an overdose that landed me in the emergency room. That week of dark and twisted hallucinations was a living hell. The out-of-control drug use had allowed demons to tightly grip with their claws. Other attempts to leave came after experiencing shame that was no longer hidden by the use of alcohol.

I began meeting often with one of the girls from the club. She invited me into her home and life. She was hooked on meth and masking trauma from her childhood. I was hooked on ecstasy and cocaine, but accepted with ease her drug of choice when we were together, which was often in those days. Truly the devil's drug, I hated what that evil substance did. Together, through invitations orchestrated in the club, we went to bachelor parties of young men who acted like animals infused with lustful greed. Near the end of my time in the industry, I felt nothing but anger for all men, especially the manager.

Coercing his way past my boundaries, that manager took what he wanted. Shame crept in after he imposed dishonor upon me. There was no one I could tell about his behavior. Besides, wasn't that just the way things worked? Somewhere in my thoughts, he was the knight in dull armor. After he committed the violation he had planned, there was a fire at his house just days later. The rumor at the club was that his house burnt down. Weeks later, I heard that another girl experienced the same violation. She was much more vocal and spoke up against him for what he had done.

All of the attempts to leave were mixed with the illusion that I was being taken care of and that the regulars were providing. I had a twisted understanding of what I thought was important. My own thoughts were deceiving me. It was almost impossible to determine what was truth and what was a lie. Time seemed to stand still in the jumbled mix of the highs, travel, feeling strung out and suddenly, six years had gone by.

The good news is that in Christ, destiny is redeemed and time is not lost. In Him, every end is a new beginning, and new beginnings come with the Refiner's fire.

My exodus from the iron furnace took the hand of a living God upon my life. It was His divine intervention that woke me up.

Consuming Fire

Fire symbolizes a number of different things, but here we will focus on holy fire and the fires of judgement as spoken of in the scriptures. I believe that the fire that came to the club manager's home was a fire from the Father. God's love was also for this man, who was entangled in the web of the industry. After all, God is a Father who is jealous in love for both His sons and His daughters.

Holy fire is pictured as a purifying agent in people's lives. In

Proverbs 17:3 (God's Word) there is a clarification of the relationship between fire and spiritual refinement: "the crucible is for refining silver and the smelter for gold, but the one who purifies hearts by fire is the Lord." In Zechariah 13:9, God brings the Israelites through the fire in order to refine them as silver is refined (see also Malachi 3:2).

Fire can be present in our lives because God's love is an all consuming fire. He is love, and He is perfect and holy. When we look at Him, His love begins to burn away everything that is not of Him. This is refining.

In Hebrews we read:

> Therefore, since we receive a kingdom which cannot be shaken, let us show gratitude, by which we may offer to God an acceptable service with reverence and awe; for our God is a consuming fire. (Hebrews 12:28-29)

Believers will receive an eternal kingdom and we are to offer devoted worship of God, by body, spirit and soul. God was and is a *consuming fire* in the sense that He desired all of the worship of the Israelites, and He desires all of our worship in how we live our lives.

Throughout the Bible we see the presence of God physically manifested as actual fire. In Genesis 15:17, God sealed His covenant with Abram by passing through the animal sacrifice as a smoking oven and a flaming torch. Throughout the travels of the Israelites, God brought protection by His fire to symbolize His guiding presence (see Exodus 13:22). And of course, many of us know the story of how God spoke to Moses from a burning bush on Mount Sinai (see Exodus 3:2).

In Deuteronomy 4:24 (God's Word), we are told that, "The LORD your God is a raging fire, a God who does not tolerate rivals." This is where we can begin to understand fire as judgement. Fire is purifying and will burn away what is perverse or idolatrous within our lives. Just look at what happened in Sodom and Gomorrah in the context of the old covenant (see Genesis 19:24). The story is evidence that fire can come as a judgment as it did upon the Egyptians.

In the last days, fire is pictured as a tool of judgement that both burns up the dross (an unwanted material or impurity that forms on the surface of molten metal) and purifies the holy. That day will make what everyone does clearly visible, because the fire will reveal it. In the final days, "He will gather His wheat into the barn, but He will burn up the chaff with unquenchable fire" (Matthew 3:12b).

The God who does not tolerate rivals, who is full of love and jealous for His Bride, was drawing me closer. He heard my cries. God desired to bring me out of the harsh tyranny of the industry that had entangled me in chords of bondage that dictated my thoughts and actions. It was finally time to leave the furnace.

Whatever It Takes

Falling to my knees upon arriving home from Miami, exhausted and strung out, I cried out to the God I had always believed in. There, in the front entryway of my apartment, I fell to the floor with the weight of what my life had become. Deep in the depths of darkness, despair became the tipping point for change. I'd had enough. After so long, I made a call to my Montana help who led me towards doing what was necessary.

Gather me as wheat into the barn, and let me not be like the husks which will be thrown into the fire. Whatever it takes, I will do.

Restoration came first in the form of out-patient treatment. While I went to counseling, there were a few final days of working at the club, but there came a moment when I was told I could no longer attend out-patient treatment because of a relapse that happened in the club.

One foot in Egypt and the other in the promise land proved to be an impossible way to live. Everything was given up after the realization that my addiction wasn't just to the drugs and alcohol, but to the strip club industry as well.

It all had to go.

Everything needed to change.

The chords of entanglements to substances and the thoughts that I needed to work at the club would eventually lessen. I had come to the point where I was willing to do whatever it would take to get better, and that meant working closely with a counselor.

The counselor I had was tough, but I needed her to be that way to help me face the reality of the life I was living. She was a prayer warrior who created and caused moments to talk about things I didn't want to talk about. Like Moses did for the Israelites, she helped me see reality while at the same time giving hope and plenty of work to bring about needed change.

What truly brought the change I needed was the One I began encountering in very tangible ways as I came to the end of myself.

I am the Lord your God, who brought you out of Egypt so that you would no longer be slaves to the Egyptians; I broke the bars of your yoke and enabled you to walk with heads held high. (Leviticus 26:13 NIV)

Most of the time, I did what I was being led to do but stubbornness would remain a character trait that stuck with me through the years. The closer I felt to the Lord, the more His fire would bring refinement. My last drink or drug was taken on July 24, 2006, but overcoming that stronghold did not happen without a fight. Prioritizing sobriety meant setting new boundaries, changing thought patterns and getting honest with myself and others.

There was a period of time during that season where I hardly associated with anyone. I spent more time encountering a living God in ways words cannot describe.

I wasn't lonely anymore.

In fact, time alone in the Word and in prayer was one of the only places I wanted to be. I began to encounter someone real, a man named Jesus who made me feel completely different. In time, I saw that He was the real hero I had always been searching for.

After the very necessary, long, out-patient treatment program, on my final drive home I felt an excitement enter my heart that was dressed in hope for change.

The moments of breakthrough to leave the club, as well as the lies of false security, were all times that led to the start of a new way of life. Life after what felt like death became a reality. The relationship with God became, for me, the way into the garden that I longed for. Like David said in Psalms, so I would begin to sing:

He brought me up out of the pit of destruction, out of the miry clay, and He set my feet upon a rock making my footsteps firm. (Psalm 40:2)

When we finally come to the end of ourselves, that moment of completely letting go to let Him lead, new life begins. What came next for me was the understanding of the reality of what happened in the Garden of Gethsemane.

Nothing would ever be the same after Gethsemane.

FIRE KEY

1. What are the things His consuming fire is burning away in your life?

2. Write and share about moments you've gone through the Refiner's fire.

3. Write about moments when you've let go and looked to God for redirection and change.

4. What are you hopeful for?

7

———

GIFTS IN GETHSEMANE

Nevertheless not My will, but Yours, be done.

Luke 22:42b NKJV

He was in the center of what looked like a small courtyard. There were no colors other than sand, dust, and the red stains of His blood. Hostility loomed in the air. The soldiers and priests circled around him like vultures closing in on their prey. The crowds, just a short distance away, began to chant in an uproar of emotion.

I quickly became aware that my focus was to be solely on Him even though there was such commotion all around. He was on His knees with a dirty cloth wrapped around His waist. His back was bare to receive the sting of the whip as it impacted a hard blow, piercing the skin barrier on His back and side. As each strong blow made its impact, His body jolted forward in excruciating pain. He whispered, *"I knew betrayal."*

Placed upon His head was a crown of thorns, twisted and sharp. The crown that pierced His head drew forth the color red.

Suddenly, another sting of the whip slashed His side, and I woke up, startled and in tears.

Salty water streamed down my face and onto my pillow like a trail of tears that came with understanding, but most of all, love for the One that I had just seen.

Everything was real.

I could see and hear all that was taking place. My senses were consumed with reality. I was right there, looking in at the courtyard, and the only thing that mattered was the Man I was looking at.

In the account leading up to His crucifixion, we are given but a glimpse of what He endured. All along, Jesus knew that being betrayed, beaten, mocked, denied by His friend Peter, and crucified was a part of the chastisement that would bring peace for the ones He had just prayed for in the garden.

Jesus came to earth and endured the agonies of Calvary instead of continuing in the joyous fellowship in His Father's immediate presence. His sole desire was to do the Father's will for the ones they both loved. The Father's will had always been love, for "Greater love has no one than this, that one lay down his life for his friends" (John 15:13). Jesus laid down His life for you and for me.

Gifts in the Garden

Gifts are a gesture of good will expressed by offering something of value to an individual without any expectation of reciprocity. A gift is given to show someone that you care. My husband knows that I receive love when he spends time with me but he also knows that he can show love by surprising me with a gift. In contrast, he receives love by words I speak as affirmations that uplift and strengthen his spirit. He also receives love through touch, which can be a kind of gift when given with honor.

Gifts can be received or rejected.

Jesus gave us gifts in the Garden of Gethsemane on His way to the cross. The Garden of Gethsemane, near the foot of the Mount of Olives, is named in the New Testament as the place where Jesus went with His disciples the night before He was crucified. The garden was well known to the disciples as the natural route from the temple to the summit of the Mount of Olives and the ridge leading to Bethany.

Jesus told His disciples, "My soul is deeply grieved to the point of death; remain here and keep watch" (Mark 14:34). Jesus went a little farther and fell to the ground as He prayed in the garden. He felt so much sorrow that He likened the feeling to death. Imagine the most sorrowful moment you've ever experienced and add a hundred or a thousand times more weight to that moment. He felt and knew sorrow.

Jesus wept.

Perhaps He didn't want His closest friends to see the sorrow He was experiencing so He went away from them. He knew He would soon be betrayed, denied and crucified. Instead of being near his closest friends, He wanted to get alone with His Father, which He often did for times of prayer.

Picture Jesus in the Garden of Gethsemane at the foot of the Mount of Olives. He walks with heavy steps, collapsing under the weight of the world, falling to the ground to pray, knowing He is about to be crucified.

Execution by crucifixion was the slowest and most humiliating of deaths. Men were flogged and then nailed naked upon a wooden cross in plain sight of the city walls. The term *excruciating* literally means "out of crucifying." Crucifixion was truly an excruciating way to die. A most painful execution, victims were sometimes left on display after their deaths as a warning to others. Jesus hung on the cross for a total of about six hours before He gave up His Spirit.

The conversation that transpired in Gethsemane between God the Father and Jesus is a conversation I believe had already been settled in understanding in their hearts.

Jesus prayed, saying, "Father, if You are willing, remove this cup from Me; yet not My will, but Yours be done" (Luke 22:42).

In His human nature, He asked for the cup to be passed from Him. The cup He referenced contained the beatings He was about to endure and being spit on, mocked, betrayed and crucified. He would even be denied by his friend Peter, the very one who had received revelation that Jesus was, in fact, the Son of God, the Christ.

The very ones He came for were about to bring betrayal.

Jesus felt pressure, pain and suffering as He prayed in Gethsemane. He certainly had to have some understanding of the pain He would go through by crucifixion as evidenced by the weight of the prayers recorded:

> And being in agony He was praying very fervently; and His sweat became like drops of blood, falling down upon the ground. (Luke 22:44)

The Mount of Olives is like an olive oil press, fitting for what took place there on the night that He prayed in agony. The word Gethsemane is derived from two Hebrew words: *gat*, which means "a place for pressing oil (or wine)" and *shemanim*, which means "oils."

Just as heavy stone slabs were lowered onto olives that had already been through the crusher earlier that day, Jesus was being crushed by the weight of all the world's sins pressing down on Him.

The heavy stone slab gradually squeezed the pulp until olive oil ran out into a pit. There, the oil was collected in jars of clay.

His blood literally fell to the ground in Gethsemane, *a place for pressing oil.* It was as if the *olive press,* The Mount of Olives, was pressing Jesus with the weight of all of the sins humanity had ever committed or would ever be committed.

Jesus's first drops of blood recorded in scripture did not come from the whip held in the hands of those He came to save, but His blood fell to the ground and soaked into the soil as He cried and prayed for you and me, taking upon Himself every sin and the weight of the world. And then, He carried it *all* to the cross.

. . .

Jesus the Lamb of God

In Sunday School I was taught that Jesus died for my sins. With this teaching, there came a lack of understanding as to why. I was taught about Jesus, His life and crucifixion, but I never really understood why He died for my sins or what that meant for me.

The sacrifice of His life for mine never made sense until my exodus from the iron furnace and my own further reading of scripture. That exodus landed me in the pages of my Bible out of what I now understand as extreme thirst. I was craving something. Many seeds of truth from the scriptures, and the Lutheran Church I had grown up in, had been planted in my spirit at a young age. Thankfully, I gravitated back towards the truth.

Roots drew me back to the living water, for when you "Train up a child in the way he should go, even when he is old he will not depart from it" (Proverbs 22:6). I am so grateful that my mom and dad gave me the gift of a Bible and brought me to Sunday School where I learned about Jesus. Even though there came a time when I stopped going to church, the scriptures stayed with me.

During my time in the furnace, my mother prayed. God gave me a dream in the midst of working at the club that I would not forget, which is just further proof that He can break through to anyone, anywhere! I dreamt that my mother came into the club to find me. In the dream I felt deep embarrassment and knew I had to hide.

Hiding comes out of intuition that what is being done is wrong. While I was seduced into the industry, I was hiding there as well.

The dream was so real, I actually asked one of the managers if someone had been in to see me. My mother later told me once I had gotten out that she had been praying with an urge to come into the club and find me. A parent's loving intuition wants their child out of harm's way and she knew I was living in harm.

As I began to study the scriptures, I discovered that accounts of animal sacrifice are found throughout Scripture because "without the shedding of blood there is no forgiveness" (Hebrews 9:22b). Animal sacrifices provided a temporary covering of sins. Animal sacrifices also foreshadowed the perfect and complete sacrifice of Jesus Christ (see Leviticus 4:35, 5:10).

God commanded the nation of Israel to perform numerous sacrifices according to certain procedures prescribed by God. First and foremost, the animal had to be spotless. The person offering the animal had to inflict death, while placing the sins of the people onto the animal. When done in faith, this sacrifice provided a temporary covering of sins.

Life is in the blood (see Leviticus 17:11).

Jesus was the perfect sacrificial Lamb of God who would literally take upon Himself the sins of all mankind. A blood sacrifice is found nowhere else and scripture tells us, "He made Him who knew no sin to be sin on our behalf, so that we might become the righteousness of God in Him" (2 Corinthians 5:21).

Of course, animal sacrifices have ended because Jesus Christ was and is the ultimate, perfect sacrifice. John the Baptist recognized this when he saw Jesus coming to be baptized and said, "Behold, the Lamb of God who takes away the sin of the world!" (John 1:29). Jesus Christ took our sin upon Himself as He endured the excruciating cross to die, and later be raised up by His Father. No grave would be able to hold perfection!

Learning about Jesus helped me understand that my sins had been nailed to the cross.

Greater love has no one than this, that one lay down his life for his friends. (John 15:13)

Jesus shed every drop of His blood to the point at which water came forth with a final piercing at His side. By accepting the gift of what Jesus Christ accomplished on the cross, through faith, we receive new life because in His death our sins are put to death but we are raised up to new life in Him. Jesus Christ is the perfect expression of God's eternal love and faithfulness, given to reconcile us to Himself (see Colossians 1:19-20).

For while we were still helpless, at the right time Christ died for the ungodly. For one will hardly die for a righteous man; though perhaps for the good man someone would dare even to die. But God demonstrates His own love toward us, in that while we were yet sinners, Christ died for us. Much more then, having now been justified by His blood, we shall be saved from the wrath of God through Him. (Romans 5:6-9)

Jesus had already laid down His life in the Garden by submitting His will to the Father out of love. It also happened to be in a garden where Adam and Eve had disobeyed God. And, not only did Jesus submit His will to the Father in the Garden of Gethsemane, praying for the ones He came for, but His lifeless body was laid in a garden tomb that could not hold Him in death.

In reading the story of His death on the cross, burial and resurrection from the grave, then His being exalted to the seat next to the Father in Heaven, I was given hope to sit with Him, *in Him*, next to the Father.

For he raised us from the dead along with Christ and seated us with him in the heavenly realms because we are united with Christ Jesus. (Ephesians 2:6 NLT)

I was being invited to receive the most precious gift. Truth became ingrained in my deepest parts, producing hope. Jesus was the bridge to all that I had been thirsting for, including love, security, safety, creativity, friendship, beauty, and so much more. That precious gift, Jesus, is available to everyone.

The Door Into the Garden

It was Mary Lennox, the character in Frances Hodgson's book *The Secret Garden,* who said, "I think I'll look for the door into the locked garden." She had hope. As a little girl, and even as a grown woman at age 25, I too searched and found what I was looking for in a man named Jesus. He became more real to me than the ones who I had known in Egypt. It was Jesus who said, "I am the gate" (John 10:9a). Jesus actually used the symbol of the door when He said He was the gate. The Greek word *thura,* usually meaning "door," can also mean "gate." The way into the garden is through Jesus Himself, and I had stepped in.

Seeking His presence, which I began to recognize and crave, I became immersed in prayer and reading the Word, participating in any activity that caused me to feel closer to Him. What followed was a response of change that radically altered my thoughts and actions. Jesus is the bread of life. When the bread of life is consumed, the life it provides forces death out. Death began to be forced out and I started displaying acts of obedience to the Father because of the love He gave me that changed both my thinking and actions.

It's up to us to accept any gift offered, and that includes the life of Christ. He said, "Behold, I stand at the door and knock; if anyone hears My voice and opens the door, I will come in to him and will dine with him, and he with Me" (Revelation 3:20). The door to the garden of my life gives entrance to who or what I choose to allow in, because love gets to choose.

In his divinely inspired book *Prayer, Why Our Words to God Matter*, author Corey Russell writes, "Jesus, fully God and fully man, is the convergence point of heaven and earth. He is the temple. In Him the two worlds are united; therefore He is the only one able to stand in the gap and reunite all that was torn apart at the fall."[3]

The more that I began to read, speak and sing the Word of God, the more I began to see myself through a lens filtered with the truth of a man named Jesus.

The value that God has placed on our lives was determined by the price that was paid. The gifts we received in Gethsemane led up to the greatest gift of all. What happened at the cross wasn't just the revelation of sin, it was the revealing of value. Whatever was hiding underneath that sin must have been of great value for heaven to go bankrupt to get us back. Jesus paid such a high price on that tree.

When I see Him there, I see my value. I need to know how much it cost to see my sin on that cross. Because when Jesus was on that cross, God determined my value.

Jesus whispers, *"You are worth dying for."*

Nothing, absolutely nothing separates you and I from the love of God. Nothing that I did separated me from God's love. Some of my actions and the actions of others caused thistles to grow, but love was chosen, and love had the power to cut those thistles. Love brings transformation that changes thoughts and actions.

God is love.

Love never forces its way. As we look at love, we become love. I hear the Lord saying:

> *I am coming back for a pure and spotless Bride who wants to marry Me. She has made herself ready and she knows love. Love forgives when betrayed. Love chooses life. Love causes transformation and My Bride is allowing Me to transform Her.*

Holy Spirit Oil

Not long after the dream of seeing Jesus there in the courtyard, I experienced what can only be described as Holy Spirit's presence of peace. Upon awakening, I heard the commandments that Moses taught the Israelites after they came out of captivity. As I heard God's commandments spoken over me, I couldn't move. To this day, I don't know if I was hearing an angel or the actual voice of God. What I do know is that the Word of God was written on my heart forever.

> Now, Israel, what does the Lord your God require from you, but to fear the Lord your God, to walk in all His ways and love Him, and to serve the Lord your God with all your heart and with all

your soul, and to keep the Lord's commandments and His statutes which I am commanding you today for your good? (Deuteronomy 1-:12-13)

It is for our good that God reminds us of His words, because a life lived in Christ means a new way that He teaches.

John the Baptist baptized with water for repentance, but he said that One would come after Him who would be more powerful. That more powerful person is Jesus Christ, and He baptizes with Holy Spirit and fire (see Matthew 3:11).

Baptism as an adult meant being led to follow Christ with the navigating guide of the Holy Spirit. It was with water that Jesus was baptized by John the Baptist. As He was baptized with water, the heavens opened and a dove appeared as a representation of the Holy Spirit. In the scriptures we also read that the Father spoke, saying, "This is My beloved Son, in whom I am well-pleased" (Matthew 3:17b). Water symbolizes righteousness, and Jesus was baptized in the water. The dove represented the Holy Spirit and the Father's voice brought approval of His Son. We too, may enter into receiving each of these treasures in response to our belief in Jesus Christ.

This is my daughter, in whom I am well pleased.

In the Old Testament, the charge was given to the sons of Israel to bring clear oil of beaten olives to make the light of their lamps burn continually (see Exodus 27:20).

Oil represents the Holy Spirit, and it is the Holy Spirit that keeps the lamps of our lives lit. It is in Matthew 25 where we learn that that Holy Spirit is the oil to light and keep the lamp burning. We don't want to be found without the oil.

Oil lamps were very small in biblical days. In fact, the amount of oil they held could be enough just for one day. This tells us that what we do with our time now makes all the difference.

The apostle John wrote, "The Holy One has anointed you, so all of you have knowledge" (1 John 2:20 God's Word), and we know the Spirit of God teaches us for, "As for you, the anointing which you received from Him abides in you, and you have no need for anyone to teach you; but as His anointing teaches you about all things, and is true and is not a lie, and just as it has taught you, you abide in Him" (1 John 2:27).

Jesus is the eternal expression of the Father's love. The life of Jesus Christ is also the embodiment of Holy Spirit. In the beginning was the Word: This Word is God's own Self, which is God's own Son. The Spirit of God was also present, hovering over the face of the water (see Genesis 1:2). The Father, Son and Holy Spirit are Trinity.

There came a time when I could do nothing else but acknowledge the gifts of Trinity. Whether or not we receive God's love as demonstrated through His Son is up to each of us individually. The more time I spent in the Word, the more I encountered pure love. I wanted my life, my lamp, to burn brightly with the only fuel that drew me closer to the heart of God.

Forgive As You Have Been Forgiven

Jesus could have stayed angry and been bitter when his cousin and friend John the Baptist was beheaded. His best friend Peter denied that he even knew him - not once, not twice, but three times in a row - just as Jesus prophesied he would. He was ridiculed, despised and misunderstood. Jesus was familiar with sorrow, yet He taught us:

> Blessed are the poor in spirit, for theirs is the
>   kingdom of heaven.
> Blessed are those who mourn, for they shall be
>   comforted.
> Blessed are the gentle, for they shall inherit the
>   earth.

> Blessed are those who hunger and thirst for
> righteousness, for they shall be satisfied.
> Blessed are the merciful, for they shall receive mercy.
> Blessed are the pure in heart, for they shall see God.
> Blessed are the peacemakers, for they shall be called
> sons of God.
> Blessed are those who have been persecuted for the
> sake of righteousness, for theirs is the kingdom
> of heaven.
> Blessed are you when people insult you and
> persecute you, and falsely say all kinds of evil
> against you because of Me.
> Rejoice and be glad, for your reward in heaven is
> great; for in the same way they persecuted the
> prophets who were before you. (Matthew 5:3-11)

In time, through my relationship with Christ, I was led to forgive those who had betrayed me. There was forgiveness given without an apology offered. While in the industry, and even long before that, I too, had brought harm that crossed boundaries. There were amends I needed to make.

I was initially inspired to choose forgiveness through a twelve-step program. That choice was reinforced by the words of scripture. At first, forgiveness felt just like words of a prayer that I wanted to believe. Forgiveness didn't make right what that person did, but it did release my heart from the anger that could have turned into bitterness. When I chose to forgive, freedom and healing came into my life.

Often times, it is up to us to make the choice not to get offended, even when we recognize someone is operating under the wrong motives. Living in offense hardens the heart to the love and light of Jesus Christ.

Eventually, I was released from praying for the individuals who had brought betrayal and violation. Forgiveness had made a way for love, and love not only impacted my life, but I know for certain that through a man named Jesus, love could impact their lives as well.

There were things I had to do for my heart to heal, like praying for someone who brought violation, even if at first the prayer was only words.

The enemy wanted to keep my heart in shame through unforgiveness and resentment, which are the devil's thistles that cut and wound deeply. But, when I held onto anger, resentment or bitterness, love was shut out. And so, in the midst of the restoration journey, forgiveness was a key that unlocked healing.

Like Jesus, what if we said to the Father, "Nevertheless, not as I will, but as You will?"

The moment Jesus spoke those words in prayer and submitted to the Father's will, an angel appeared to bring strength. That in itself tells us about the moment we choose to do the right thing by responding to Holy Spirit's leading. Sometimes the hardest thing to do is to love in spite of being provoked at a moment when we could easily get offended or snap back. Not only are there angels there to assist the ones who prove to be Jesus's disciples, but there is also the strength and power of the helper, who is the Holy Spirit.

He must increase, but I must decrease, for fierce love shows honor in thought and action. We do not want to be conformed to the image of this world, but instead, choose to have our minds renewed to "prove what the will of God is, that which is good and acceptable and perfect" (Romans 12:2b).

May the cry of our hearts be, "Teach me your way, Lord, that I may rely on your faithfulness, give me an undivided heart, that I may fear (*worship*) your name" (Psalm 86:11 NIV). Here, both the old and the new covenants agree that the true worship of God is essentially internal. This true worship is a matter of the heart, rooted in the knowledge of and obedience to the revealed Word of God, through a life that chooses love!

The Olive Tree

Studies have confirmed that there are eight olive trees that are siblings of the olive trees that could have been in the Garden of Gethsemane the night that Jesus prayed. The trees have identical DNA, indicating that they came from cuttings made when branches were pruned and then grafted into a new tree, all originally belonging to the same mother tree.

This finding supports the idea that a particular olive tree was specifically chosen by God for this purpose, perhaps because it was believed to have "witnessed" the night of Jesus's agony. Oil is still being pressed from the fruit of those eight ancient and gnarled olive trees and that oil is still lighting the fire that leads the way into the garden, along a path pruned by the vinedresser Himself.

Like Jesus who said, "My food is to do the will of Him who sent Me and to accomplish His work" (John 4:25), may we also say, "My will is to do The Father's will."

Treasure was given as a gift in the garden that day for those who would believe. The Garden of Gethsemane, at the foot of the Mount of Olives, pressed the garden with olive trees where Jesus prayed and was later betrayed. Just as pressure caused Him to cry out, the pressures we face in this life can cause us to cry out as we train the human spirit to choose love and honor. This process that unites Heaven and Earth is like the molding that a gem goes through.

God's love is the kind of life of love that shows us how to live. As we submit out of love to His perfect leading, there are treasures that produce hope in abundance. In difficult times we can:

> ...exult in our tribulations, knowing that tribulation brings about perseverance; and perseverance, proven character; and proven character, hope; and hope does not disappoint, because the love of God has been poured out within our hearts through the Holy Spirit who was given to us. (Romans 5:3b-5)

It is no wonder that for those of us who believe, we too experience being "pressed on every side, but not crushed; perplexed, but not in despair; persecuted, but not abandoned; struck down, but not destroyed" (2 Corinthians 4:8-9 NIV).

> We always carry around in our body the death of Jesus, so that the life of Jesus may also be revealed in our body. For we who are alive are always being given over to death for Jesus' sake, so that his life may also be revealed in our mortal body. (2 Corinthians 4:10-11 NIV)

Being consigned to death, which might resemble being persecuted, means to choose love, life and honor, even in the face of hate, death and dishonor. In the places of pressure, when we choose love, we are lifted up. In the moments of betrayal, when we choose love, His light and love lifts us up.

It was in a garden that Christ gave us entrance into the Kingdom by His life, death and resurrection. It was also in a garden where man and woman stumbled in temptation, and a garden was the place where Jesus's body was laid, and where He later rose in victory. Although the locations are different, the truth that all of this happened in a garden is part of God's perfect design.

Jesus prayed in agony in the same place where scriptures tell us He will come to stand as King on the Mount of Olives. Because Jesus submitted to His Father's will for the sake of love in a low place, when He comes back His feet will stand on the Mount of Olives, east of Jerusalem, on a high place.

From the low place to the high place - from the pit to the palace! Jesus prayed to His Father in a garden:

> I do not ask on behalf of these alone, but for those also who believe in Me through their word; that they may all be one; even as You, Father, are in Me and I in You, that they also may be in Us, so that the world may believe that You sent Me. The glory which You have given Me I have given to them, that they may be one, just as We are one; I in them and You in Me, that they may be perfected in unity, so that the world may know that You sent Me,

and loved them, even as You have loved Me. Father, I desire that they also, whom You have given Me, be with Me where I am, so that they may see My glory which You have given Me, for You loved Me before the foundation of the world. (John 17:20-24)

Jesus showed us that we too can follow the Father's will even when it is difficult. His life was an example to those of us who would follow and obey Him (see Hebrews 5:9). Perhaps this conversation between the Father and the Son was written to encourage us to see the reality of a struggle, to teach us how to *love not our lives, even unto death*, and to demonstrate what it looks like submit to the Father's will.

Jesus knew that His Father could do anything, yet, for the sake of showing the extent of their love, He demonstrated the greatest love ever manifested. The perfect Lamb of God laid down His life for the joy set before Him - you and me.

Waking up from the dream, I realized I had seen but a moment of what Jesus endured for the joy that lay before Him (see Hebrews 12:2). On my side was a large marking that had not been there when I had gone to sleep the evening before. There was no pain, and eventually the mark faded in time. In the natural mind, devoid of faith, I could have thought up any number of reasons for that mark appearing. In my spirit, knowing what happened in the dream, faith told me that I shared in a moment of His sufferings.

Can we become so close that we share in His joy and sufferings? Can we become so close that we have the privilege of being persecuted when speaking truth instead of saying what the world says? Can we become one as the scriptures tell us that we are to do?

But He was pierced through for our transgressions, He was crushed for our iniquities; the chastening for our well-being fell upon Him, and by His scourging we are healed. (Isaiah 53:5)

I hear Jesus saying, *"Beloved, If this was only for you, I would do this. Beloved, will you choose love?"*

Once again, I would dance and sing like when I was a little girl, however, this time I would dance in freedom to show honor, and not for any man in movements of seduction. No longer would dance be controlled by any devil presenting as a puppet master for gain in an empire of lust and greed.

Love was the reason Jesus prayed in the Garden of Gethsemane. Love was also the reason He submitted to the Father's good will. For me, love was the reason for actions made in faith to exit Egypt once and for all. I didn't realize it at the time, but love was leading me.

The exodus from Egypt had just begun because there are many destiny moments on the road to promise for those of us who dare to take a leap of faith.

FORGIVENESS KEY

1. What gifts do you want to receive that you've read about in Chapter Seven? How do you know you've received these gifts?

2. Write and talk about a time when you chose to do the Father's will - the right thing - instead of acting out of your flesh/human nature.

3. Is there someone you are holding onto anger or resentment towards that you can forgive?

4. Have you ever been persecuted for your faith? If so, how did you respond?

5. Read out loud and meditate on John 17:20-25.

8

EXODUS JUMP

*Have I not commanded you? Be strong and courageous! Do not
tremble or be dismayed, for the Lord your God is with you
wherever you go.*

Joshua 1:9

With the hard ground beneath my bare feet, I could feel each pebble
as I tiptoed through the dirt. I was in some remote location, off-site
from our compound, for several days of a bootcamp that came as a
surprise. It had taken me several tries and much encouragement
from those I could see below who had already made the jump.

I didn't realize this was what I had signed up for. Apparently
team building means being put through a test in order to function
properly as a unified group. I was ready to take a break after
hauling the trunk of a very large tree for several miles in the hot
summer sun. Carrying that tree trunk wasn't done alone, but none-
the-less, it was a challenge coordinating how to move a tree down a
dirt path road with others. We each had an idea of how it could be

done. Finally, after each strong-willed person shared their idea of how we could accomplish our task, we settled on a solution and ventured on.

We set up camp with little to no supplies while being held to a time limit. What came next was building a bridge with tires and rope across a river, propelling off rocks, and sitting in the wilderness - alone in the pitch black night. To this day I'm fairly certain a lion or large animal of some kind passed me by as I hunkered down close to a tree and kept my eyes on the only light I could see, the stars. Out of fear, others had grouped together after only an hour. I could hear friends gathering to find one another but was too frightened to even move. Seeking God there, in that place, was the only way I could breathe.

Each activity in that three days took courage, and even though I caught my first ever case of heat stroke, it was all worth it.

Back up on top of that large rock, I peered over the edge. Like small specks in the water, all I could see were the tops of their heads. One who had already made the jump kept count before my plummet into the cold water. As some kind of encouragement to get me to jump, he yelled upwards in excitement, "One.... Two... Three!" I took a deep breath before launching off the rock into the water below.

Somewhere in South Africa, outside of Pretoria, my feet left a place of comfort for the unfamiliar. Even though it was uncomfortable, I knew this was a jump that I wanted to make. I was leaving the old life behind, jumping into the new, no matter how frightened. If I could get through Egypt, I could jump into this new life of faith and sobriety - the day life and not the night life.

Like the Israelites, I left what I knew, not necessarily knowing the road ahead. The Exodus jump took trust and courage, one step at a time, one day at a time, to learn the voice of the One who called me out.

The Greek word *exodus* means "the road out." Total dependence on God is what it took for me to take the road out of the industry as well as the lifestyle that had come along with it.

The Israelites followed a promise for something better as they followed Moses into new lands. I followed Jesus, led by the Holy Spirit, Who imparted courage and trust for a new way of life, into a new land.

The Departure

The departure, otherwise known as the Exodus of the Israelites from slavery in Egypt, is symbolic of an individual leaving a life caught up in entanglements. Moses, a foreshadow of the Messiah, was sent by God to deliver the Israelites from their captors who profited from their labor.

The process, otherwise known as the restoration journey towards the promised land, was necessary for the Israelites. The restoration process was also necessary for me and, just like the Israelites, it was not an easy road.

> Now when Pharaoh had let the people go, God did not lead them by the way of the land of the Philistines, even though it was near; for God said, 'The people might change their minds when they see war, and return to Egypt.' Hence God led the people around by the way of the wilderness to the Red Sea; and the sons of Israel went up in martial array from the land of Egypt. (Exodus 13:17-18)

In a roundabout way, God has been leading many of us through the desert so that we learn to seek Him, hear His voice, and find the only water that will quench thirst. God wanted me to learn His voice. He also wanted me to heal. Had I known the reality of some of the wars ahead, it's possible I may have turned back to the furnace. The furnace wasn't just the strip club, it was also the drugs and alcohol. God took me to Africa so I could detox from Egypt.

The 13th Floor

We gathered together near the main hall of the compound. The night sky shone brightly above as it covered us in a canopy of stars. Kathleen began to give direction. She was the dance instructor in charge of choreographing dances for the gospel play productions that many of us would be involved in.

Of course, God would have it that I was chosen for the dance team.

That night of gathering was not a night for choreography, but for the freedom to move and heal. The only instruction was to allow the emotions that emerged from song to be demonstrated in movements of dance. As a young girl, I had taken many dance lessons, including jazz, tap and ballet. I've always loved dance. To be able to move in expression causes life and healing. My dance was stolen in the midnight hour, but it was also recovered in the midnight hour in the heart of Africa.

As the song began I danced to break free. All of me - body, spirit and soul - moved in expression to heal from all that had happened. I danced to honor God with a new found joy that I felt. I also danced to express grief from the heartache that June 27th had brought. In those movements of grief, I danced. In movements of hope, His love brought a breath of life that I felt throughout all of me.

For the first time ever, the only One that I focused on in that moment was God. Nothing else mattered. His love invaded the depths of me and I truly felt loved - body, spirit and soul - all of me.

Getting the opportunity to join the *The 13th Floor Arts Ministry* there in South Africa brought needed healing. It was among true brothers and sisters in Christ where I learned to jump. Learning to jump meant learning to trust God's leadership and be vulnerable when He was leading me to speak up about Egypt.

I encountered aspects of God that I had longed for, deep down inside. I learned how to express the new found freedom I felt through song, dance and painting. Scripture teachings, outreach to serve others and utilizing God-given talents were all a part of a plan of restoration. We worshiped and preformed the gospel message in a way that youth could comprehend through the arts. Through others, God taught me about His love. I learned how to share my story for the first time in front of new people who all carried testimonies of their own. Listening to the stories of others brought healing.

It was there, outside of Pretoria, where I learned about the night watch from the Holy Spirit. Many times I was woken in the night to pray with specific details. I didn't comprehend at the time, but God was teaching me to pray during the time that I had once given to the devil. The midnight has since become a time of prayer and intercession, as well as outreach back into the places I was taken out of.

One evening, I heard the sound of a girl screaming. From my room, and out of my bed, I launched into the hallway to investigate. Unable to locate where the screaming was coming from, I paced the halls and prayed.

The next day, one of the girls shared that she had been having terrible nightmares. There were things going on in the night that the elder staff eventually disclosed with me after I shared my burden of midnight intercession. Spirits were literally harassing some as they tried to sleep. Soon after getting the opportunity to pray with one of my elders, God gave me a dream. He woke me up to pray specifically for the girl who had been screaming in the night. Once again, I was led into the hallway by Holy Spirit to declare the Word of God in intercession for those who slept. Something changed that night and I was able to go back to sleep.

Thanks to wisdom from the Lord, a prayer team that wouldn't give up, and learning about the night watch, the nightmares ceased.

So began the night watch in the midnight hour.

That time in the 13th Floor gave me a glimpse of the truth necessary for women coming out of exploitation to heal. We must learn to move our bodies in honor and not seduction. The *Exodus Jump* meant learning to move my body in a way that honored God. He gave me courage unlike any drug or toxic love that I had previously known. Learning to live and dance for Him, an audience of One, is freedom.

. . .

Superstitious 13 or a Two-Fold Promise

The number 13 has been known as a superstitious kind of negative number, and understandably so, but there is more than meets the eye to this number. The beast as described in Revelation 13 speaks of the enemy. The Elite, also known as the Illuminati, have 13 levels of Masonic hierarchy. The dragon, a symbol for satan, is found 13 times in Revelation. Satan is behind all rebellion against God and His elect. He also tries to take what is sacred and significant and bring distortion. For example, if we look at the ideal for the number six (man expressing sacrificial love in relationship to God) and the number seven (divine rest, completeness, and reverence), we see both love and unity together. Clearly, 6 + 7=13.

Digging deep into rabbinical teaching, the number 13 is actually a positive number. Hebraically, *ahava*, "love," equals 13. The root of ahava is *hava*, which means "to give." It also shares a root with the word, *ahav*, which means "to nurture, or to devote completely to another." Marriage can have ahava love. So the essence of the Hebrew word ahava is not an emotion, it's an action and it can be found in scriptures such as Deuteronomy, when God's love is spoken of:

> The Lord did not set His love on you nor choose you because you were more in number than any of the peoples, for you were the fewest of all peoples, but because the Lord loved you and kept the oath which He swore to your forefathers, the Lord brought you out by a mighty hand and redeemed you from the house of slavery, from the hand of Pharaoh king of Egypt. (Deuteronomy 7:7-8)

God's ahava love is also spoken of in Song of Solomon 2:4, "His banner over me is love."

Another use of the number 13 is found in Exodus. In Exodus we find a positive connotation of the number 13: God taught Moses the secret of His thirteen attributes of mercy in Exodus 34.

Also, consider Abraham. At 99 years old God's promise came for Abraham, but it wasn't until a season of waiting and testing was completed that the promise came about. At 86 years old, Abraham tried to bring about God's promise on his own. Instead of allowing his wife Sarai, who was old in age, to become pregnant as God said she would, Abraham slept with Hagar at Sarai's suggestion. God promised Abraham that it was Sarai who would give birth to a son, but he tried to bring about the promise himself. 99 minus 86 equals 13. Therefore, it was 13 years between the promise given and the promise manifested.

Instead of trying to make things happen ourselves, we are to trust and wait on God's perfect timing.

A different way of looking at the number 13 is by viewing it as a promise that involves man and God. The promise brings about a great change.

The invasion of Jericho is stamped with the number 13. The city was marched around for six straight days, and on the seventh day it was marched around seven times, making the total number of times around 13. It took man (symbolized by 6), cooperating with God (symbolized by 7) for the promise to unfold. Taking Jericho was a two-fold promise that involved man and of course, God's leading. Man needed to listen to God's instructions, believe and follow Him. The only way great change happens is when the strategies of God are manifested.

In his book *Prayer: Why Our Words to God Matter*, Corey Russell writes, "...God has always operated in partnership with His people. He has a dream, He grips men and women with the spirit of revelation, they join their hearts with His in intercession, and then His will is manifested in the earth."₄

Joshua listened to the exact instruction of the Lord to take the city of Jericho in his younger years. In Joshua 13:1, long after Joshua led the Israelites into a battle through the gate of the city to take

Jericho after the walls fell down, God tells him, "very much of the land remains to be *possessed*" (emphasis mine).

It is time to take back the spaces and the places where the enemy has set up camp.

There is land, and places of influence yet to be taken in these days. For some of us that means going back to what we came out of to bring a message of hope. The 13th floor has to do with entering into the spaces and the places that have yet to be taken. My friend Cat French once said, "The sons and daughters must come out of Babylon before its swift and complete destruction." She's right and the only way to do that is to follow the best leading of the Holy Spirit.

The Gates

God gave Abraham a mighty promise that his seed would flourish: "indeed I will greatly bless you, and I will greatly multiply your seed as the stars of the heavens and as the sand which is on the seashore; and your seed shall *possess the gate of their enemies*" (Genesis 22:17, emphasis mine). Abraham's seed was Joshua. You and I are also Abraham's seed. In other words, we will conquer as victorious children of God, because of whose we are, and the covenant blessing that God made with Abraham.

Galatians 3:29 declares, "And if you belong to Christ, then you are Abraham's descendants, heirs according to promise." As God's heir, the promise given to Abraham is the same promise that belongs to you and me.

The Hebrew words for *possess* mean "to control, to have power over, or to have authority over." Abraham's descendants are to possess and have authority over the gates.

Gates are symbolic of spiritual power and authority. Gates speak of rule. Gates also speak of the place of counsel and of *justice*. Proverbs talks about gates in a number of passages, referring to that place where people would sit to receive counsel or advice from the elders in the gates. Those who sat in the gates were people who knew counsel and understood laws and regulations.

Princes and judges sat at the gates and discharged their duties. Court was held there and disputes were settled. Priests and prophets delivered discourses, admonitions, prophecies, and counsel at the gate (see 2 Kings 7:1, 22:10; Nehemiah 8:1-3; Jeremiah 17:19). The people gathered at the gate - or in the courtyard of the gate - for conversation, to share local news, and for discussions of a variety of subjects.

Everyone who passed through the city had to enter and exit through the gate. Because the gate was where people would come and go, this was also a good place for a marketplace. The gate became a symbol of strength, power, and dominion but it was also the weakest point of defense and therefore heavily defended.

Watchtowers were constructed above the corners of the gates as lookout posts. These towers were places where watchmen could see when an enemy was approaching and call the city to alert. At night the gates were closed, barred and guarded, secured by locks with big keys.

To possess the gate was to possess the city!

There are a few things we can learn from this. First, we can control who (or what) enters in through our gates. Second, we are being taught to possess the gates of our enemies.

God was teaching me how to live in and by His Spirit, to go into the "gates" to bring change, and He does the same for every believer. Consider the gates of our time as the places of influence, whether business and education, media and the arts, and/or the government.

Many of us are called to the gates to bring change.

My ongoing and deepening relationship with God was a training ground for things to come. Years later, during a time of worship, I saw those close to me suited up in their armor like soldiers. We were standing at a very large gate. The enemy was on the other side. All of a sudden, the foot of God came down and smashed the gates as we moved forward as a unified army.

A two-fold promise between man and God brings about the greatest change. It takes trust and courage to move forward in His divine timing.

Courage In Action

There are moments in life when we just know it's time to jump, even if it takes several promptings to finally go for it. The exodus jump means jumping into something new, even if it means going in a roundabout way. Persistent thoughts with an inclination to leave the old behind is oftentimes God's leading. When we can't see the entire picture but move anyway, we practice faith. Faith believes and hopes for the best even though everything is not seen.

The Israelites had to have faith to take a new way.

While the initial directions for the journey may seem straightforward, we are often rerouted just like the Israelites so we will learn and grow. We must adapt to hearing God's voice and following His ways in preparation towards receiving inheritance as responsible children of God.

Mustering up the courage to take a leap of faith meant revolution. A choice to no longer spend time with those who were using drugs and alcohol was part of my exodus jump. Choosing to not be alone with a man in my sober journey was also a part of the exodus jump. I didn't want to continue wrestling with the same thistles and thorns, so boundaries were set.

Another leap of faith came the moment I secured an honoring job working at a youth treatment center a few short months after going through treatment myself. The first check I received was significantly less than what I was used to making, but holding that check in my hand gave me a sense of accomplishment without the taste of guilt. I felt proud of getting to work on time and being able to encourage those young teens.

As time went on, I had to learn to break old mindsets. Times I was lacking in finances would come with thoughts to go back to the club. Digging into scripture, praying and speaking the Word all helped break those old thought patterns.

Another exodus jump came at the acceptance of an invitation to a Bible study, even though I felt uncomfortable and thought praying out loud with others was crazy. Working through the steps of a certain program helped launch me into a greater understanding of a new life.

The new way gave plenty of opportunities to show courage, even if that meant speaking up to protect my growing faith. Although a certain sponsor was significantly helpful for a time, once she argued with me about Jesus, I knew our time working through the steps together needed to cease. When I prayed for mentors who would teach out of the Bible, God was faithful in answering that prayer.

Jesus became more real than anything else.

Reading the Word of God became my favorite thing to do. Thoughts about myself began to change. Hope grew like ivy cascading over the walls of this new garden that I had entered. It was Jesus who gave me the courage to get up and go to work. Eventually, I went back to college after saying yes to that incredible opportunity in Africa that brought healing.

Follow His Lead

The Israelites' lack of belief in God's good instructions held them back from what otherwise would have been a 40 day journey into the Promised Land. Disobedience and complaining kept the Israelites in the wilderness for 40 years. It was during that time that they learned what they needed in order to move forward.

It took obedience on my part to move in the promptings to leave Egypt as well. Trying out for the arts ministry, going to college, and even leaving the career I went to college for to start a ministry meant taking steps of courage.

I still don't know exactly where I was in South Africa when I jumped off that rock and into the water. What I do know, is that moment of courage resembled what I would need to move forward instead of going back to Egypt. Exodus from Egypt meant trusting the One who was now leading me in a good way. Leaping off that rock was both thrilling and scary, but once I finally hit the water, I realized it was the jump I needed to make. Leaving Egypt was just the beginning of the journey. Nothing would ever be the same.

COURAGE KEY

1. What scriptures can you find about courage? Write out three of them in your journal.

2. When have you taken leaps of faith that took courage?

3. What is the two-fold promise? What could that mean for you?

4. What helped the Israelites move forward in their new journey and what held them back?

9

THE DREAM OF THE BRIDE

Do not interpretations belong to God? Tell me your dreams.

Genesis 40:8b NIV

The straight road was in front of me. All I had to do was get there.

As I walked forward, going to the place I knew I needed to go, I caught a glimpse of a tall, dark man wearing a black coat.

Trying not to pay him any attention, I kept my focus forward, walking towards the straight way while trying to ignore the feeling of fear that was welling up inside. Fear was a distraction. He was trying to get my attention from a side street that was not on my path. The road I was trying to get to was only three, maybe four blocks away. The man picked up his pace and instantly I knew it would be a life or death moment if I did not get away from him.

Before I could run, I was caught near the side street where he was standing. I tried to look away, but he stood directly in front of me. There was no getting away. His eyes were the darkest black I've ever seen. In an instant, he grabbed me.

Everything went dark.

The next thing I remember was waking up in a small room on a bed. Although I was in a delirious state, intoxicated by some substance, I noticed that there was a girl across from me tied to another single bed. She was either sleeping or blacked out. She also had bruises and cuts all over her body. As I opened my mouth to speak, I realized my voice was gone. Feeling alarmed that I had no voice, tears streamed down my face as again, I tried to speak. Not only was my voice gone, but I was not able to get up from the bed. Looking down at the floor, I saw different colors and kinds of shoes. The shoes represented the girls who had been there before me. Feeling confused and desperate for help, I shuffled around on the bed, hoping to find a phone.

In the next scene of the dream, although still unable to get up, I had a phone in my hand. The only number I could remember was my dad's number. When he picked up the phone and said hello, I couldn't respond.

I had no voice.

The dream flashed to a final scene.

I was in an underground shop in a white wedding dress. The tall, dark man with the black eyes was laughing as he ordered one of his helpers to make sure and hold me tightly so I could not get away. Frantic, I tried moving out of his tight grip. Looking into his eyes for any amount of humanity, morality or compassion, I caught a glimpse of something good. For a second he saw me...*all* of me. The compassion I saw immediately vanished at the sound of his taskmaster. It was like he was under some kind of spell.

All around the room there were men in line to purchase me like I was some sort of commodity, void of soul or spirit. The man with the black eyes looked at me and laughed, saying, "Which one do you want?" I felt confused and tried even more to get away. Every time I opened my mouth to speak up, I found I was without a voice, which only added to the already existing fear.

In a final scene of the dream there was a white piece of paper in front of me. There, before my eyes, a drawing of a church building appeared. Underneath the church were the words *"Tell Ruth."*

The meaning of the awakening dream has been revealed over the years. The solutions to come out of captivity continue to bring awakening. Before going into the meaning of the dream and its relevance to us, let's take a look at the importance of our dreams.

The Source of the Dream

Dreams are significant. To understand dreams and interpret them correctly is not only important, but it's necessary. There is so much to be understood about dreams. There are entire books written just on the topic.

Dreams are responsible for many of the greatest inventions of mankind. In a dream, James Watson got the idea of DNA's double helix spiral. We can thank Elias Howe for the invention of the sewing machine, another idea that came from a dream. The periodic table was given to Dimitri Mendeleev in a dream. Of great significance are the dreams that have been given to those who know they are called to intercede.

New Testament dreams often presented inspired, divine knowledge. For example, specific instructions and warnings were given to Mary's husband Joseph, the earthly father of Jesus. And in The Old Testament the Israelites knew a dream could be a prophetic message from God. God is the same, and He still speaks through dreams.

Although we can receive dreams from God, we can also have "soulish" dreams as well as dreams that are demonically crafted. The Bible speaks of *midheaven* (see Revelation 8:13; 14:6; 9:17) and *third heaven* (2 Corinthians 12:2), which implies that there is a *first heaven*. The *second heaven* is where the demonic realm is set up. Third heaven is where God is enthroned.

There may be times where the Holy Spirit gives insight into the plans or schemes of the evil one through a dream. When this happens, it is for the purpose of prayer, because with Christ inside you have access to the mind of Christ. With your sword (the Word of God) and ability to create an atmosphere that honors God (through song, creativity, worshiping, etc), you have the ability to cancel the schemes of the devil.

In James and Michal Ann Goll's book *Dream Language*, the authors give an explanation of the kinds of dreams that people can receive and they share the biblical truth that it is God who gives dreams for specific purposes. God is supernatural and He communicates to His people supernaturally. Goll teaches the following as three different kinds of "transmitters" for dreams:

- God Himself: God is a personal God who transmits dreams to individuals. These, of course, are spiritual dreams inspired by the Holy Spirit.
- Natural Man: Natural or "soulish" dreams and visions are produced by the natural processes of our mind, will, and emotions. Dreaming is a normal part of the human brain function when in a deep sleep state. Sights, sounds, smells, and other sensory stimuli from the day provide the raw materials from which our brains create natural dreams. Sometimes, if we are not careful, we can confuse a natural dream with a dream from God.
- Demonic Darkness: False and occultic dreams fall into this category. These are dreams that are demonically inspired, deceitfully crafted by evil agents. ₅

Lessons from Joseph and Daniel

While dreams are important, equally significant is correct interpretation.

Joseph the dreamer was given a dream that his brothers did not like to hear. Although he was sold into slavery, it was God who quickly elevated him to a place of favor in Pharaoh's eyes. While Joseph was sitting in prison, it was God who was setting up the perfect circumstances for him to interpret the dreams for Pharaoh's chief cupbearer and baker. Coincidentally, they each had been thrown into prison for offending their royal master. Was this a coincidence or a God-Incident?

After dreaming their troubling dreams, Joseph asked them each why they looked so worried. When they explained their dreams, Joseph spoke with wise words to bring the interpretation. He was divinely inspired to set up his own elevation process. Joseph had no idea what would come next. He simply kept a good attitude and spoke of God even while in a difficult circumstance.

In Genesis Jospeh proclaimed, "Do not interpretations belong to God? Tell it to me, please" (Genesis 40:8b).

Joseph eventually came out of prison and interpreted the dreams of Pharaoh. At that time, Pharaoh was accustomed to calling on the magicians and the wise men of Egypt for help in this area. None of the sorcerers could interpret Pharaoh's dreams. After Joseph gave correct interpretation of Pharaoh's dream, making sure to credit God, Pharaoh elevated Joseph to prime minster of Egypt. Joseph interpreted dreams with wisdom, looking to the One who was the only wise source. Joseph pointed to God and gave Him the credit before all the others.

The book of Daniel is also jam-packed with revelation and insight on dreams. Just like in Genesis, where Pharaoh's magicians were unable to interpret his dream, in the book of Daniel, King Nebuchadnezzar's sorcerers were also unable to bring interpretation.

Daniel brought interpretation to the king's dreams with wisdom we can put into practice. First of all, Daniel recognized who gave the dream, and made sure to speak to this truth. Before Daniel interpreted the dream, he went through a process to make sure he and his friends were not subject to the harsh judgment decreed by the king. Daniel, along with his friends and others known to the king as "wise men," were to be executed.

It was Daniel who, "handled the situation with wisdom and discretion" (see Daniel 2:14), not the sorcerers. Daniel found out what was going on by asking for more information. He then *went at once* to see the king, asking him for time to interpret the dream that mystified the magicians and sorcerers. Then, Daniel went home and *told his friends,* urging them to, "request compassion from the God of heaven concerning this mystery, so that Daniel and his friends would not be destroyed with the rest of the wise men of Babylon" (Daniel 2:18).

Daniel had his tribe, those who he trusted and was able to pray with. When I've had impactful dreams over the years, I've first written them down, then sought God for understanding, and in some cases have shared the dream with my husband or a woman I trust. Interpretation can come from others, but it's important to be discerning about who we share our dreams with.

Daniel and his friends sought God together. This tribe of friends lived in the Babylonian culture but were determined not to defile themselves. Basically, they lived in such a way that brought honor to God while they lived in a corrupt culture. The Babylonian government had chosen Daniel for royal service to the king, and yet he made clear, healthy boundaries. It was God who gave these young men the unusual ability to understand literature and wisdom. And it was God who gave Daniel the special ability to interpret visions and dreams (see Daniel 1:17).

The secret of the dream was revealed to Daniel in a vision. Once he understood the dream, he *praised and worshiped* God.

> Daniel said, "Let the name of God be blessed forever and ever, for wisdom and power belong to Him. It is He who changes the times and the epochs; He removes kings and establishes kings; He gives wisdom to wise men and knowledge to men of understanding. It is He who reveals the profound and hidden things; He knows what is in the darkness, and the light dwells with Him. To You, O God of my fathers, I give thanks and praise, for You have given me wisdom and power; even now You have made known to me what we requested of You, for You have made known to us the king's matter." (Daniel 2:20-23)

Daniel interpreted the dream in detail for the king and made sure to say, "However, there is a God in heaven who reveals mysteries, and He has made known to King Nebuchadnezzar what will take place in the latter days" (Daniel 2:28a). Daniel went on to interpret several other dreams for the king. Nebuchadnezzar experienced God's power, and that led to him worshiping God.

Daniel recognized the *urgency* and *took action* with courage by approaching the king; Daniel told his friends and together they prayed; God responded; they worshiped. Before the interpretation came, Daniel was already a worshiper. He honored God in the way that he lived.

The ministry my husband and I have founded with our good friends is the result of several dreams, confirmed words and a ton of miracle moments. Action169 came from the scripture in Acts 16:9 where Paul was given a dream to go and help those who were crying out for help in Macedonia. What I love about this verse is that immediately after Paul had the vision, he took action.

Write the Vision

For years, before I answered the call to step into the dream of destiny, it was the dream of the bride who couldn't speak that shaped many of my prayers, studies and footsteps. Jumping out of Egypt and into the promised land meant joining myself with God the Father, the One who gives dreams for purpose.

Papa Lou Engle, a spiritual father in our nation, said it best when referring to a relationship with God: "If you hang around the 'Dream King,' you get into His dream stream, you join yourself to His dream team, and you do the Martin Luther King thing."

To "do the Martin Luther King thing" is to stand in a place of intercession to bring change, like fighting for the civil liberties of others. Justice is one of God's attributes. Justice flows out of His holiness and in relationship to Him. In relationship with God, we begin to think and act according to what is true, moral and ethical. Awakening to justice is awakening to who God is, and thus, who we are as His children. The psalmist recognized and wrote about God's justice: "Righteousness and justice are the foundation of Your throne; Lovingkindness and truth go before You" (Psalm 89:14). In Hosea we are told, "Therefore, return to your God, observe kindness and justice, and wait for your God continually" (Hosea 12:6).

Dreams may come to awaken us to justice for ourselves or for others.

Everybody dreams, but not everybody remembers their dreams. Developing the habit of writing your dreams down means you are being a good steward. You may find that as you better steward the dreams you are given you'll receive more. In writing my dreams down, praying and asking God for clarity, not only has there been understanding, but many more dreams of awakening have occurred.

Keeping journals and writing brings understanding to my world, thoughts, and most importantly to what God is saying and revealing. In Habakuk we are given a perfect example of the significance of not only writing, but waiting on God:

> I will stand on my guard post and station myself on the rampart;
> And I will keep watch to see what He will speak to me, and how I
> may reply when I am reproved. Then the Lord answered me and
> said, "Record the vision and inscribe it on tablets, that the one
> who reads it may run. For the vision is yet for the appointed time;
> It hastens toward the goal and it will not fail. Though it
> tarries, wait for it; For it will certainly come, it will not delay."
> (Habakkuk 2:1-3)

Dreams come with all sorts of symbolism and meaning, which is why it is so important to write them down, pray, and listen to what the Holy Spirit is saying.

Dream interpretation does not belong to the occult.

Dream interpretation belongs to the Body of Christ, because God created us to dream. He speaks through dreams and visions. The soulish dreams can even give further understanding of your soul (mind, will and emotions) and body condition. The Holy Spirit in you can intercede for you even when you are sleeping: "In the same way the Spirit also helps our weakness; for we do not know how to pray as we should, but the Spirit Himself intercedes for us with groanings too deep for words" (Romans 8:26).

You must learn about your dream life.

"And it shall be in the last days," God says, "That I will pour forth of My Spirit on all mankind; And your sons and your daughters shall prophesy, and your young men shall see visions, and your old men shall dream dreams." (Acts 2:17)

The Seduction into False Royalty

Children are incredible dreamers.

When I was young, as well as wanting my own secret garden, I wanted to be a singer. Not only did I actually have dreams about singing, but I would walk around the house singing into a pretend microphone. The desire to sing was God-given and the enemy wanted to twist and destroy that God-given dream.

Singers need to have a voice.

Singers who declare and trumpet the sounds of God's Word in worship and adoration towards Him must have a voice. Those who want to share their stories or testimonies of redemption also need to have a voice.

The dream of the bride showed her without voice, unable to speak. She was also caught in some dark web of deceit as a body commodity, intoxicated by substances, and being seduced with temptation by the deceiver.

Notice in the dream how the enemy turned to her to ask, "Which one do you want?" The Bride of Christ can be tempted by seduction and choices, and eventually silence becomes betrayal.

In another dream that was given to me not long after the dream of the bride, the Lord exposed evil's attempt again. Dark figures were attempting to push me out on a stage while trying to place a purple fur coat on me. Purple is a color of royalty, but these dark figures were trying to cause a false royalty that brings attention to self. The people on stage were being cheered for by an audience that was under a spell. On the stage I saw Miley Cyrus being controlled by strings like she was puppet. Her tongue protruded from her mouth as she danced provocatively in actions that mimicked perverse sex. As I sought to resist being pushed out onto that stage, I woke up. After waking up, I prayed.

When there is resistance to what is perverse, there comes awakening.

The dream came long before Miley's movie award performance where she depicted acts of sex while singing about being able to, "Party and do whatever we want."

The Dream of the Bride Revealed

As evidenced by both alarming dreams, the plans of the enemy are to seduce, sedate and then silence. Not only was I in a drug-induced state, but I felt frantic throughout the dream because I couldn't speak. Besides being auctioned off like I was a body commodity void of a spirit or soul, I too, was the one being seduced when the man with the black eyes said to me, "Which one do you want?"

The strategy of evil is not only to silence the bride, but to hijack her voice. Speaking up and speaking out is key. From the dreams, which led to years of relevant prayer for the Body of Christ with a unified team, it's clear that God is ringing the alarms for us to:

1. Understand God-given dreams and visions
2. Awaken by verbalizing an out-loud agreement with the Word of God
3. Recognize entanglements that seduce, sedate and silence
4. Get onto the straight road

Before Mary Lenox found the key to her garden, she had to learn to speak up. She also had to learn that there were those who wanted to discourage her by telling her there was no key or garden to find.

I had to learn there were safe people that I could share things with who would lead me into prayer so my focus would be on Jesus. Like Joseph, there were dreams that would bring change.

As I pondered these things, I heard the Lord whisper:

You, dear one, are clothed in a robe of righteousness that I give you. Your robe is dignity and honor. You are a daughter of the living God, capable of mighty moves of justice and greats acts of love. You are precious and honored in My sight, and I love you. Speak up and let your voice be heard so that you are not held in captivity by silence. I am the One who draws you onto the straight road with lovingkindness and a strong arm. Know what My Word says, and follow Me.

DREAM KEY

1. What scriptures can you find about dreaming? Write out three of them in your journal.

2. What kind of dreams have you had recently? If you haven't already, ask God for understanding.

3. What was the dream of the bride about in chapter nine? What were the related solutions?

4. For further understanding of your dreams, I recommend reading: *Dream Language*, by James and Michael Ann Goll.

10

LIVING WATER

But whoever drinks of the water that I will give him shall never thirst; but the water that I will give him will become in him a well of water springing up to eternal life.

John 4:14

The purple amethyst rock that sat on the shelf in the living room when I was young didn't actually have a sobering effect for any of us. The only kind of influence to bring about sobriety is the Lord, Himself, who is likened to the stability of a rock throughout scripture.

The word rock is used about 24 times in the book of Psalms in reference to God. In Psalm 18:2, when David is delivered from the hand of his enemy, he proclaims, "The Lord is my rock, and my fortress and my deliverer, my God, my rock, in whom I will take refuge, my shield, and the horn of my salvation, my stronghold." God is a rock in the sense that He is the Lord of the Armies who is strong. He is the Holy God, also referred to as *Elohim* and *Adonai*, meaning "master." God is a master, author, and provider (see Genesis 18:2, 40:1; Samuel 1:15; Exodus 21:1-6)

A rock can also be an obstacle that causes one to stumble. In Romans 9:32-33, Paul presents us with a stone that he called a stone that causes men to stumble and a rock that makes them fall. This stone or rock he is referring to is Jesus. He is our Messiah-stone, the Savior and Judge of the world who loves justice and hates injustice. With grace He stands as a stone to meet us in love. Because of Him, we can enjoy the everlasting rest of eternal life and peace, now. Jesus is truly a rock of safety to those who receive Him, but a stumbling block to those who reject Him.

During the wilderness wandering of the Israelites as they traveled to the promised land, God caused water to flow from a rock. The rock was in a place where there was thirsty ground, scorpions, and serpents. In Deuteronomy 8:15, by God's instruction, Moses is reported to have "brought water for you out of the rock of flint." In this example of water pouring forth from a rock in the wilderness, we are catching a glimpse of a prophetic moment that foreshadows Jesus being the only One who can quench thirst.

Addiction can be like those scorpions and serpents.

A young man once said to me, "I just want to get high and the urge won't go away, so I may as well give in and use." Not long after this statement he was headed back to prison for violating parole from the use of substances. He believed the lie that there was no way out. Not only was he dealing with an addiction, but without realizing it, he was really looking for love.

The definition of addiction can be boiled down to compulsive use of a substance (or engagement in an activity) despite ongoing negative consequences.

There was a time when all I wanted to do was get high, even though life had become wrought with consequences. The use became an escape which progressed into full-blown addiction. A long-kept secret only fueled my use. Where there was addiction, there was shame, for they are one-in-the-same.

Things had to get bad enough, dark enough, and black enough

for me to want to reach towards the living water and the only rock that could sustain me. Sobriety had to be a priority, and that meant getting honest with myself and others.

Living Water or Dead Water

It was with *water* that Jesus was baptized by John the Baptist. As he was baptized with water, the heavens opened and a dove appeared as a representation of the Holy Spirit. The Father spoke saying, "This is my Son in whom I am well-pleased" (Matthew 3:17).

An example was set that day that rebirth, or being born again from death to life in Christ, comes with cleansing water. John the Baptist, Jesus and the crowds who gathered that day were at the Jordan, in the wilderness. It would be safe to say the symbolism of water meant cleansing and a resurrection to new life in Jesus Christ. John the Baptist, Jesus' cousin, compared his ministry of water baptism to that of Jesus who baptizes with the Holy Spirit (see John 1:33; Acts 1:5).

In Israel, during the time of the biblical account of the Samaritan woman at the well, women went out either early in the morning or later in the evening to fill their cisterns with water. It was too hot to go in the daytime, but it was in the middle of the day that the Samaritan women went out for water. It's likely she went during a time where there were less women who might tease and ridicule her.

Jesus never looked with condemnation towards those He met and He certainly does not look with condemnation on us. The scriptures tell us, "there is now no condemnation for those who are in Christ Jesus" (Romans 8:1). While the Samaritan woman, whose name was Photina, was at a well during the hot summer sun of midday, Jesus met her there. He was there in the place of her bidding. He asked her for water, which came as a surprise for it was not customary for Jewish people to talk to Samaritans. When she gave Jesus water, He answered and said to her, "If you knew the gift of God, and who it is who says to you, 'Give Me a drink,' you would have asked Him, and He would have given you living water" (John 4:10). Jesus goes on to further explain:

> Everyone who drinks of this water will thirst again; but whoever drinks of the water that I will give him shall never thirst; but the water that I will give him will become in him a well of water springing up to eternal life. (John 4:13-14)

The world's way of quenching thirst and God's way are very different. In her excitement of meeting the Messiah, Photina went and told the townspeople that she had met the Christ. For this act, she is sometimes recognized as the first to proclaim the Gospel of Christ. Think about going from hiding in shame because of a known lifestyle to proclaiming Jesus to the very ones you used to hide from. Some of us, including myself, are doing this very same thing.

When we get a taste of the living water, the dead water just does not satisfy anymore. King David knew about thirst for living water when he wrote, "As a deer pants for the water brooks, so my soul pants for you, O God" (Psalm 42:1). He found an activity that allowed him to drink from the living water. David worshiped with his harp.

Finding activities that feed the spirit can be likened to drinking living water. When I start writing, painting, playing piano, hiking in the woods or creating things that bring honor, life begins to well up within me. During activities of creativity, Holy Spirit moves freely if not quenched. We were created by a Creator, and in every one of us there is a characteristic to create something. Your creativity may be released while making something of beauty, building, or designing.

Creating creates connection with the Creator!

Peace as living water flows from the Word of God in moments of creating, which can be an act of worship. Think about this: Jesus said, "the water that I will give him will become in him a *well of water springing up to eternal life.*" We can grow spiritually in times of creating to "be like a watered garden, and like a spring of water whose waters do not fail" (Isaiah 58:11b).

Wells of water, like the living water that Jesus spoke of when He was teaching the woman at the well, are available to each of us. Not only is the living water available, but it connects us to eternal life.

Pharmakia to Sedate

Some people are able to stop after drinking half a glass of wine, or perhaps a glass. I was never that person. It's all or none, and it's always been all or none in most endeavors. Most of the people I've met who have struggled with substance use are really some of the most creative, driven and courageous people. Once they pursue sobriety and restoration with that same all-or-nothing mentality, there is no stopping them.

We get our English word pharmacy from the Greek word *pharmakia*, which literally means "drugs." Pharmakia appears five times in the New Testament (see Galatians 5:20; Revelation 9:21, 18:23, 21:8, and 22:15) and is translated into our english Bible as either "witchcraft, sorceries, magic, enchantments or spells." In each of the five passages, pharmakia, or drugs is listed as a work of the flesh of man as opposed to the Spirit of God working in us.

This reveals a lot about any mind or mood-altering substance, including prescription pills such as opioids or CNS (Central Nervous System) depressants (barbiturates and benzodiazepines like Xanax). Anyone who has dabbled with methamphetamines knows this is the devil's drug. The entire point of this drug is literally to kill, steal and destroy.

In Galatians, Paul teaches to act according to the Holy Spirit we must "walk by the Spirit, and you will not carry out the desire of the flesh. For the flesh sets its desire against the Spirit, and the Spirit against the flesh; for these are in opposition to one another, so that you may not do the things that you please" (Galatians 5:16-17). Furthermore, we are given a list of the deeds of the flesh: "immorality, impurity, sensuality, idolatry, *sorcery*, enmities, strife, jealousy, outbursts of anger, disputes, dissensions, factions, envying, *drunkenness,* carousing, and things like these, of which I forewarn you, just as I have forewarned you, that those who practice such things will not inherit the kingdom of God" (Galatians 5:19b-21 *emphasis mine*). For me, removing alcohol and other toxins was a start towards dealing with the rest of those behaviors.

Neurotransmitters in the brain called dopamine and serotonin are released to cause a feel good effect when drugs are taken. These chemicals are naturally a part of the brain. A problem is created when drugs are taken that cause them to be released, because there is then a depletion of those feel-good happy chemicals. The person using begins to chase the same effect by taking more drugs over a progression of time so more dopamine and serotonin will be released.

Anyone who has experienced drug or alcohol abuse or dependence knows what it is like to chase the high. Eventually, the brain actually stops producing dopamine receptors all together. Cocaine, meth and especially MDMA are all physiologically and *spiritually* addictive, and they are all very dangerous. Eventually, the consequences outweigh the momentary effects of feeling good.

One of the reasons I used cocaine and MDMA in a progressive manner is because of how the drugs made me feel. Chasing the high meant I would use more of the substance to try and get the same effect. I became hooked quickly due to the predisposition towards alcoholism that was passed on at birth. That generational pattern has since been dealt with and broken.

Instead of practicing continuing the drug or alcohol use, I began practicing being sober. This meant setting boundaries, getting honest, and getting in the Word of God. These choices helped diffuse and eventually eliminate cravings caused by triggers.

Sober Child of God or Alcoholic

Through my experience, study of scriptures and work with clients, I've learned that the success of treating alcoholism or drug addiction comes first from the person truly having had enough. Then, if that person becomes willing to do what it takes to get sober, working in conjunction with the Lord while being delivered from the very real entanglements of addiction, that person can be free of the desire to use substances. Of course, practicing daily, ongoing action steps is a necessary part of the journey.

It wouldn't have mattered much if someone told me I had a problem. I had to hit my own rock bottom and experience having had enough myself.

Full eradication and prevention of alcoholism and drug addiction is available, and while there are 12 step programs that are certainly helpful, complete eradication comes from the healer Himself, Jesus Christ. Choosing some other form of a high power will not take away thirst.

In the beginning of my walk in sobriety, I labeled myself as an addict because that was what I was taught. The more I dug into scripture, the more I learned the truth of how God saw me and no longer could I keep calling myself an addict. Acknowledging addiction and admitting that things have gotten out of control can still be possible while also declaring the truth of what God says. Denying there is a problem is an aspect of the illness - that's not what I am talking about. No longer did I desire to declare sickness or an active addiction over myself and so I changed my verbiage. To use again, for me, would mean inviting those spirits of addiction right back into my life.

Declaring truth brings freedom.

While we do live in the world, we do not wage war as the world does. To acknowledge there is problem is one thing, but to speak out a disease or addiction over oneself is oppositional to what scripture says. Agree with what God says about you, and know that He is not speaking over you the words alcoholic or addict. Speak this declaration aloud:

Hi, my name is _____, and I am a sober, set-free, child of God.
Seated in Christ with the Holy Spirit in me, I'll use my sword,

which is the Word of God, because I do not wage war in the flesh, according to the flesh. The weapons of my warfare are not the weapons of the world. Instead, my weapon has divine power to demolish strongholds, tear down arguments, and every presumption that sets itself up against the knowledge of God. My weapon, the Word of God, will take captive every thought to make it obedient to Christ.

Dealing with changing thought patterns and receiving deliverance of the spirits connected with pharmakia brings complete freedom because of Jesus Christ. Declarations over self that line up with scripture bring truth and freedom. Working through the steps of a specific program can be helpful as long as it lines up with scripture. The urge to drink alcohol or use drugs can be completely taken away.

The Good News

We were each created with a hunger and thirst to experience, create and know love. The world's way to get high is only temporary and always produces some kind of trouble or unrest that will eventually lead to poor health and ultimately, death. We were created to know His experiential love, creativity and wonder.

We desire and long for experience, acceptance and love. As we drink from the living water we become empowered to produce the fruit of the Spirit.

But the fruit of the Spirit is love, joy, peace, patience, kindness, goodness, faithfulness, gentleness, self-control; against such things there is no law. Now those who belong to Christ Jesus have crucified the flesh with its passions and desires. (Galatians 5:22-24)

The Old Testament teaches the temple was a place that was built for the Lord's presence to dwell. Now, in the new covenant sealed and signed by Jesus Christ, His presence dwells *within us*. In 2 Chronicles we learn about the Lord's temple being filled with a cloud of God's glory and how the priests could not perform their service because of the cloud. In the book of Acts 2:15, people thought the followers of Jesus were drunk on wine because of the way they were acting, but they were not drunk on wine, they were filled with the Holy Spirit.

In the Song of Solomon, love is likened to wine and God's love is referred to as being better than wine. This reveals that addictions are rooted in the need for love. When someone uses a drug or abuses alcohol despite the negative consequences, they are searching for a kind of love that can only be satisfied in a relationship with God.

After drinking a little wine, a relaxed feeling follows, but God's presence causes a better experience of peace without the hangover and regret of bad choices. At times I've referred to His presence as intoxicating because of the incredible, life-changing encounters. Following His lead has meant making better choices all together, and those choices have led to healing and wholeness. What good news to know that the Holy Spirit can boost dopamine and serotonin levels.

You have anointed my head with oil; my cup overflows. (Psalm 23:5b)

My Cup Overflows

The oil, a symbol for Holy Spirit, represents intimacy with God. Through the gift of God's Spirit, we can understand not just the parables Jesus spoke in, but we can also experience guidance as we walk through this life. The Spirit gives life, for:

The Helper, the Holy Spirit, whom the Father will send in My name, He will teach you all things, and bring to your remembrance all that I said to you. (John 14:26)

All believers are new creations in Christ. If you're not sure about the Holy Spirit, or whether you've been baptized in His Spirit, ask God. Ask Him to baptize you in His Spirit. Nothing will ever be the same again.

In the book of Acts the disciples were doing just as they were instructed. "Peter said to them, 'Repent, and each of you be baptized in the name of Jesus Christ for the forgiveness of your sins; *and you will receive the gift of the Holy Spirit*'" (Acts 2:38, emphasis mine). The word *repent* means "to turn the other way or to go in a different direction."

Holy Spirit and the living Word of God enable us to be honest and make changes. We can declare the Word of God, speaking the living Word out loud and be empowered towards doing what is healthy, good and right.

Empowered to Choose Well

To feel empowered, or to empower another person, is to promote the idea of self-efficacy. Self-efficacy is knowing you have the ability to make a choice that will have a good outcome. When someone is taking action by feeling empowered they might exhibit confidence in their ability to achieve a good result. Self-efficacy effects every endeavor.

When feeling empowered, we are motivated towards a greater responsibility and authority in our own lives to make good, healthy choices. If we better understand the choices that are available to us and what the outcome could mean, we may be more likely to make a good decision.

If we act on our feelings instead of God's word, we are headed for trouble. The good news is that we can receive wise Holy Spirit-inspired instruction. But, where does this new strength to carry out better choices come from? To understand, we must look at the root meaning of the word empowerment.

The Greek verb *endunamoó* (en-doo-nam-ó-o) means "to empower." In Greek, *dunamoó* means "to make strong and enable."

The strength spoken of in the word endunamoó, is not a self-made strength, but a strength that is given or shared. Another definition of the word *endunamoó* is "I fill with power, strengthen, make strong." Notice the definition illustrates there is power coming from someone else, "*I* fill with power." The particular combination of *en* and *dunamoo* (empowered) is only found in biblical related Greek.

Strength is the Greek word *ischus*. Ischus has a lot of implications, from health to moral endowment. It is "applied capacity, otherwise known as the ability to do well." The Greek word *kratos* is "might." This is a word meaning "power available for action." It doesn't imply that the action takes place, only that the power is ready to be used when needed.

Jesus supplies the available power. How do we know this? Because in Matthew 28:18, we are told by Jesus Himself that, "All power is given to me in heaven and on earth."

In the book of Matthew we read about the woman who sought desperately to get to Jesus. She had faith that just touching His robe would bring healing to her.

And a woman who had been suffering from a hemorrhage for twelve years, came up behind Him and touched the fringe of His cloak; for she was saying to herself, "If I only touch His garment, I will get well." But Jesus turning and seeing her said, "Daughter, take courage; your faith has made you well." At once the woman was made well. (Matthew 9:20-22)

The woman was healed because Jesus Himself is healing. She had faith in Him. It is Christ who "dwells in our hearts through faith" (see Ephesians 3:17). He provides us with strength, healing and wisdom and enables us to make ongoing healthy choices.

In 2 Corinthians 12:9, God reminds us of His imparted strength: "My grace is sufficient for you, for my power is made perfect in weakness." We find it is not our own strength, but His strength that enables and empowers us. It is His might that is available to us so that we can act in wisdom, wellness, love and strength. His might provides the needed capacity for the ultimate empowerment.

Examples of Empowerment:

…with respect to the promise of God, he did not waver in unbelief but grew strong in faith, giving glory to God. (Romans 4:20)

Finally, be strong in the Lord and in the strength of His might. (Ephesians 6:10)

I can do all things through Him who strengthens me. (Philippians 4:13)

I thank Christ Jesus our Lord, who has strengthened me, because He considered me faithful, putting me into service, even though I was formerly a blasphemer and a persecutor and a violent aggressor. Yet I was shown mercy because I acted ignorantly in unbelief; and the grace of our Lord was more than abundant, with the faith and love which are found in Christ Jesus. (1 Timothy 1:12-14)

You therefore, my son, be strong in the grace that is in Christ Jesus. (2 Timothy 2:1)

But the Lord stood with me and strengthened me, so that through me the proclamation might be fully accomplished, and that all the Gentiles might hear; and I was rescued out of the lion's mouth. (2 Timothy 4:17)

Speaking Words of Life and Love

In Proverbs 18:21 scripture tells us, "The power of life and death are in the tongue." Another form of empowerment as living water is to speak life. Living Words of life cause good change. Our Creator spoke life with just one word! In James we are told:

> Look at the ships also, though they are so great and are driven by strong winds, are still directed by a very small rudder wherever the inclination of the pilot desires. So also the tongue is a small part of the body, and yet it boasts of great things. See how great a forest is set aflame by such a small fire! And the tongue is a fire, the very world of iniquity; the tongue is set among our members as that which defiles the entire body, and sets on fire the course of our life, and is set on fire by hell. (James 3:4-6)

A spoken word is an audible expression of sound that carries frequencies. Dr. Masaru Emoto discovered that crystals formed in frozen water reveal changes when specific, spoken words are directed toward them. Water exposed to loving words shows brilliant, beautiful, complex and complete snowflake patterns. In contrast, when the water is exposed to negative words, it forms incomplete, asymmetrical, dull patterns.

Not only do we need to speak life and love over ourselves, but also over one another. May we be people who show honor in our thoughts, words and deeds. Getting into the Word of God to declare truth can assist in this practice. We have many other things to talk about than one another, so let's practice praying, speaking life, and talking about what is excellent.

In Philippians 4:8 we are told, "Whatever is true, whatever is noble, whatever is right, whatever is pure, whatever is lovely, whatever is admirable—if anything is excellent or praiseworthy—think about such things." Let's not gossip, spread rumors or speak harshly about one another. The serpent, who is the accuser of the brethren, whispered lies of deceit into Eve's ears. We join forces with the accuser when we whisper into the ears of others.

Daughters who honor seek to empower. Daughters of honor, when they hear a sister talk about another, will intuitively know how to turn the conversation. If any words are spoken of one another, let them be good words of honor and love. Let's encourage and uplift one another all the more in a world where bullying leaves wounds of rejection.

We are meant to cheer one another on. Fixing our attention on God, we are changed from the inside out. We bring love and honor towards one another. Unlike the culture around us, which is always seeking to drag us down to its level of immaturity, God brings out our best. In turn, we can choose to see, call out, and draw out the best in others. Honor is now being restored into the Bride of Christ. No longer will she speak harshly about her sister, but she will honor her with her words, as does her Father in Heaven.

Journaling and Writing to Heal

In Habakuk 2:2, the Lord said to Habakuk, "Write the vision; make it plain on tablets, so he may run who reads it." The benefits of writing and journaling do not only solidify the vision, but the activity itself is healing for those who cultivate the habit. Writing has been one of the greatest keys of restoration in my journey and it's a key I encourage clients to start right away.

Developing the habit of writing will make way for a better understanding of self, goals and most importantly, what the Lord is saying. Learn to organize your thoughts, think with clarity and go deeper in your relationship with God. Express your ideas and get creative. Journaling is also an outlet to process emotions and increase self-awareness.

Journaling is a route to healing - emotionally, physically, and psychologically. Improved immune function has been seen amongst participants of writing exercises. Stress often comes from emotions and overthinking hypotheticals, but when we translate an experience into language, we make the experience understandable. In doing so, we free ourselves from mentally being tangled in traumas.

There's a strong connection between happiness and mindfulness, a byproduct of writing. Journaling literally causes mindfulness. Past frustrations and future anxieties lose their edge in the present moment. Writing calls a wandering mind to attention, from passivity to actively engaging with the Spirit.

Journal Topics

Setting time aside to write, whether morning or evening, is an act of discipline - and discipline begets discipline. Journaling is for all of us, not just some of us. The following questions are great journal topics:

- What has gone well for you this week?
- What scriptures have been highlighted to you?
- What is God teaching you in the scriptures?
- What project are you creating or designing?
- What are you looking forward to?
- What is a lesson that you learned this week?
- What are 5-10 things that you are grateful for?
- What healthy choices did you make today?

For more ideas on journal prompts or healing activities, please refer to "Best Care Practices" which can be found on the Action169 website.

Living Water Brings Peace

Trinity connects the beginning of your life to the water that flows "from the throne of God and of the lamb" (see Revelation 22:2). Life is available to those of us who choose to drink from that living water. We choose to drink from the living water or the dead water.

We have a choice as to whether the garden of our lives will

bloom from living water or be poisoned from toxic water. Too much dead water and we dull our senses and become numb.

Over time, the realization came that I'd rather paint, play music, work out at the gym, or spend my evenings reading a good book than spend my days and nights in a haze. Daughters, step away from that crowd that spends their weekends drunk. We were made for so much more!

God is absolutely crazy in love with us, wanting to give experience after experience, glory to glory, moments that are worth more than nights in a bar.

Shalom is a Hebrew word that means "completeness, soundness, welfare, peace." Shalom is taken from the root word *shalam*, meaning "to be safe in mind, body, or estate." Shalom can be experienced during quiet times of rest or while doing creative activities during times of worship. Shalom rest is the kind of peace that Jesus is speaking of in John when He says:

> Peace I leave with you; My peace I give to you; not as the world gives do I give to you. Do not let your heart be troubled, nor let it be fearful. (John 14:27)

Caring for self by drinking from the living water is to experience the shalom peace that Jesus speaks of. Draw near to Him and He will draw near to you. Find the activities that feed your spirit. Discover the actions that draw you into a place of rest. Peace like living water flows from His throne into the heart that takes refuge in His presence.

Before inviting Jesus into my heart, I didn't have the kind of peace that I do now. He is the shalom peace, the living water that I had been searching for all along.

Let those who are thirsty come! (see Revelation 22:17)

LIVING WATER KEY

1. What scriptures speak of living water? Write them down and say each one out loud.

2. What activities help you drink from living water?

3. In what ways can addiction be a counterfeit?

4. Begin to cultivate the habit of journaling. Utilize the questions in this chapter to write in your own journal.

11

FOCUS IN THE SEASONS

*How beautiful you are, my darling, how beautiful you are! Your
eyes are like doves behind your veil.*

Song of Songs 4:1a

My new restoration journey has come with many lessons. The first
relationship I became involved in was two years after getting sober
and filled with the Holy Spirit. Some of the greatest things God will
do in our lives happen when we are in transition. In my transition
time I became enrolled in the school of the Spirit, which came with
lessons on seasons, focus and foxes.

Foxes are nocturnal creatures, which means they are active at
night. They move quickly; a fox can run at a speed of about 23 miles
per hour in a short time frame. Foxes are believed to be a very intel-
ligent but also have the stereotype of being sneaky. A fox prefers to
be out on his or her own and will eat most anything to survive.

Before the "fox" moved in, my singleness was not only necessary, but also enjoyable. I was getting back in touch with playing

piano, painting, and writing - all of the things that caused life to rise up in me. Most importantly, I was spending more time with the Lord and in His Word. I was learning to truly take care of myself - no drugs, no alcohol and no temporary comfort from the presence of a man.

While the self-care and healthy activities continued, it was this new guy who stirred up a familiar feeling. He captured my attention and pursued me outside of a small group of friends who got together for Bible study. We prayed together and read the Bible, things that were new to me in the scope of a relationship. We began to spend more time together, and that time was often alone - just the two of us.

I liked being pursued, which brought back familiar feelings. My focus changed. Even though I began to sense conflict in my soul, I liked his attention.

With a growing awareness of boundaries and a healthy sensitivity to listen to my body and spirit, each time we would begin to be physically intimate, I would feel nauseous. What we were doing was not honoring to ourselves, to our future spouses, or to each other. Because God is all-knowing, and because He gave me the Holy Spirit, even in moments of beginning to kiss and become close, my soul and spirit would react.

This time, I was sober and listening.

If we are quiet enough without dulling our senses, we can hear exactly what God is calling us to do.

God knew this man was not my husband. He knew who my husband would be, and He knew I was starting to become intimate with someone whom I would not be spending my life with.

To understand where foxes fit into this story, we'll look to the scriptures.

Foxes ruin what is good. In Song of Songs 2:15, the lovers in the story want to make sure there are no foxes in their life: "Catch the foxes for us, the little foxes that spoil the vineyards, for our vineyards are in blossom." When the bride exclaims, "catch for us the foxes the foxes which spoil the vineyard," the bridegroom leaves.

He did not want his bride to be focussed on the foxes but wanted his bride to be focussed on him. The story can be likened to how God feels about us, His Bride. The relationship itself was the fox that took my focus off Jesus.

My desire to find a partner for connection and affection was God-given. It was the action of becoming intimate with a man who was not yet my husband that was not safe.

While I experienced the turmoil of emotions, my mother was given a dream that she shared with me for clarity. She knew she was supposed to tell me about the dream. Interestingly, I had been praying for a sign and even took time to get away at our family's cabin to figure things out. In the midst of attempting to break off the relationship, as challenging as it was, the dream confirmed the focus on this "fox" (relationship) was not for my best.

Because my focus had changed, God was seeking to get my attention to guide me out of that relationship. While there were some godly qualities that I had been attracted to in this man, it was a dangerous and cunning relationship, which God led me out of. Sometimes we need to change our perspective for the sake of fulfilling destiny. I needed to change mine.

Before learning more about the fox, let's look at the eagle, a creature who has a focused perspective.

Sitting through a teaching from a respected Native American friend, I heard an incredible story about the female eagle. It was explained that she is very wise when it comes to choosing a mate. In fact, it has everything to do with the strength of the mate and whether or not he'll be able to catch their young should they fall from the nest too soon. Basically, the female eagle checks to see if he's got the character to be a father.

During the final days in the whirlwind of that relationship, I made a list of character traits I desired in a mate. Learning from the Bible, I listed godly and ungodly qualities. Then, I prayed and let go. That man was never intended to be my husband.

· · ·

Meeting Destiny

Corey came into my life when I wasn't looking for a mate. In fact, upon first encounter I thought he was kind of strange because he was always so happy. We met while ministering to youth, and little did we know, God was orchestrating destiny.

It was God's design, not my own, that Corey and I would meet. It was his relationship with the Lord that was most attractive. The story of our meeting came with many divine confirmations. For the first time ever, I was pursued with honor and integrity. God opened my eyes and my heart to Corey. Our first kiss was a week before we were married. We've been married since 2009 and celebrate sobriety birthdays, a love for the outdoors, and most importantly, love for Jesus.

All along, God always knew this was the man I would marry.

Get the Foxes Out

A fox can ruin what is being built in groups of friends, ministries, the church, or even in a relationship. We are called not to focus on the fox, but to set our eyes on one thing, as the Psalmist would say:

> One thing I have asked from the Lord, that I shall seek: That I may dwell in the house of the Lord all the days of my life, to behold the beauty of the Lord and to meditate in His temple. (Psalm 27:4)

A fox is a distraction and can even come in the form of a person, likely filled with ill intent for personal gain. Foxes can also be likened to sinful appetites and passions. Bitterness, envy, gossip, slander, and anger are all examples of foxes.

In the Bible, Sampson burned 300 foxes at the tail. Perhaps it's time to burn up gossip and slander, along with the passions the lead to heartbreak. Don't let the foxes spoil a good thing. Remember what Solomon said - they come to ruin the vineyard. A vineyard filled with beautiful, fragrant blossoms is like a covenant of love with the Bridegroom, Jesus. The little foxes point to all the enemies and adverse circumstances which threaten to destroy love and honor.

Have you ever heard a fox bark or, even worse, the vixens scream? It's not a pleasant sound. You don't want foxes around making unwanted noise.

It's important to realize that our struggle is never against a person, although it may seem that way. It is the accuser of the brethren (satan) who seeks to stir things up. We never want to agree with the accuser when he slanders a person. We are each made in God's image and we have to fight the good fight with love, boundaries and wisdom from the Lord.

Know who your enemy is.

Keep the focus on Jesus.

Remember, "For our struggle is not against flesh and blood, but against the rulers, against the powers, against the world forces of this darkness, against the spiritual forces of wickedness in the heavenly places" (Ephesians 6:12). With that said, remember the Spirit that lives on the inside (Holy Spirit) is greater than the spirit that lives in the world (satan).

If the Lord shows you a fox, deal with it first by praying. Know that it is good and necessary to set boundaries. Watch your tongue so as not to invite the foxes yourself. A fox is easily roused in temper and loves to battle. Typically, foxes want the last word, so let them have it. A fox will usually have selfish motives. Be wise and lock the door to the foxes.

So, how do we lock the door and "burn the foxes?"

Well, that's about focus.

Focus Like a Dove

Doves have binocular vision. This means they can only focus on one thing at a time. Usually, that focus is their mate. Because of this, doves have been called "love birds."

In the book Song of Songs, we learn how the Bridegroom expresses His love for His bride:

How beautiful you are, my darling! Oh, how beautiful! Your eyes behind your veil are doves. (Song of Songs 4:1)

Given that God speaks of His love's eyes being like dove's eyes seems to allude to the fact that she only has eyes for Him. She moves when He moves. She does what she sees Him doing and knows that it is good. She does not turn or get distracted, looking to the right or to the left. He is the only one she sees, implying that His leading is what matters most. She does not waiver nor turn from her purpose - to follow her Beloved wherever He might lead is her priority.

Don't get me wrong - this doesn't mean we are not to get married or refrain from having "dove's eyes" for our marriage partner. Marriage, the relationship between a man and woman in covenant, is blessed by God. In Song of Songs we see the beauty of a committed love (ahava), a love that is protected by God-given boundaries.

Sexual intercourse was designed by God as a holy means of celebrating love, producing children and experiencing pleasure within the boundaries of marriage. While my faith-based walk deepened, I learned that sexual intimacy outside of marriage violates God's purpose for sex and marriage. The sexual relationships I had outside of the covenant of marriage did not foster blessing or health but instead invited havoc, heartbreak from soul ties, and dishonor. There are entire books just on this topic, and much can be found in scripture to support these truths.

As a Christian, I didn't want the world, including the media, to have more of an influence on me than the Word of God. The Lord was leading me to keep focus and get rid of the foxes. Going through the narrow gate has to do with letting the Lord actually be Lord. In the areas of sex, sexuality and intimacy I needed some direction. God's Word brought the best direction. He led me to say no to the pursuits of one who would not be my husband because He knew there was danger and heartache.

Summer Romance

Over time, I became infatuated with learning about God. I asked Him for a hunger for His Word, and most especially, His presence.

One particular summer afternoon, I got out a piece of paper and asked Him to reveal truths about Himself. Scriptures flooded my thoughts. With my Bible open to find each of the scriptures, I wrote down the verses Holy Spirit highlighted. During this time, I started to feel the presence of God, which came with feelings of peace. By His Spirit, I was led all over the Bible as He pointed out verses and stories so that I could learn about Him. The writing and drawings on my paper became an expression of His character.

As I laid back to see the clouds outside my window, His presence surrounded me. The Lord reminded me of times that were difficult, but revealed that He was right there all along. I spoke out words of praise to acknowledge His faithfulness and all that He had done. This became a time of focused worship.

When thinking of His goodness and all I had to be grateful for, I couldn't help but praise Him. God is a rewarder of those who seek Him.

In seeking Him, He takes care of the foxes.

Someone once made the comparison to me that if I was willing to drive in a blizzard for drugs, or travel to a different state to work in a club, then surely I could give my time and energy towards sobriety, self-care and my faith. Surely, I could give singleness a chance so I could grow in faith, learn boundaries and keep my focus. Seeking Him with the same intensity and zeal, I discovered treasures instead of shame.

Our atonement to God is a life for a life - our life for the life of the Son of God. Therefore, we each come to Him, one at a time. We are each one-of-a-kind and He is totally in love with us. And because we are each unique, created in the image of God, we can each say with confidence, "I am God's daughter and He loves me."

When I have struggled to believe Truth, I've sang it out loud instead.

The truth of God's goodness, along with healing from trauma, permeates the spirit with song.

Gomer Allured into the Wilderness

For many of us, when coming out of things like addiction, vile sexual exploits, being exploited or even being the exploiter, we've had moments like Gomer.

Recall that Gomer was the wife to Hosea. Hosea's life became an example of God's feelings towards His beloved people, His bride Israel, because Gomer left her husband several times. When she left him, she went back to a place that was familiar to her, although it was harmful. She actually prostituted herself. Many of us may have thought of, or even followed through with, going back to what is not good for us and putting ourselves back into the grips of what once brought oppression.

In the Book of Hosea, God told Hosea to take a wife who would give herself away to other lovers. This action to betroth a woman who would later prostitute herself into slavery represented how the people of Israel were unfaithful, turning to idols like Baal.

As Hosea's bride, Gomer committed adultery.

God's bride, His covenant people, committed idolatry with Baal.

To reiterate what was written in chapter four, the story of Hosea's love for Gomer is the story of God's love for the wayward Israelites. The addictions - whether it be to drugs, alcohol, money or men - are each like Israel's foreign gods, also called idols. The story depicts how we can choose the way of disobedience that inevitably will lead to suffering. In spite of the fact that I was coerced into the sex industry, my entangled decisions to turn to that next high or to place money over morality were all connected to serving a different master. As the Israelites searched for fulfillment in the wrong places, we have also looked for comfort in the wrong places.

Until we are ready to fully surrender, we seek after other lovers down harmful paths. But, when we humble ourselves and seek God, He is more than willing to meet us in the place of trouble to lead us towards safety, healing and wellness on a good path. God was there with me all along, even in the depths of drug use and turning to other comforters that left me miserable.

The heartbreaking account of Hosea and his efforts to preserve his marriage with Gomer reflect the grief God expresses over the people He loves and has done so much for. His love is a jealous love, for He longs for the relationship with the ones He wonderfully created. He also seeks to lead us into a good space and place, a good land, a *promised land*.

In mercy, God allures His bride back to Himself as described in the book of Hosea. Although already mentioned in a previous chapter, to drive home the point, let's take another look at the verses:

> Therefore, behold, I will allure her, bring her into the wilderness and speak kindly to her. Then I will give her her vineyards from there, and the valley of Achor as a door of hope. And she will sing there as in the days of her youth, as in the day when she came up from the land of Egypt. (Hosea 2:14-15)

God, in His divine love, will use the most loving persuasions to allure us to the places where we acknowledge Him. In the valley of trouble and sorrow, there can be a door of hope. When I acknowledged that I needed Him, that my way wasn't working, and that I would follow His leading, there came restoration and hope.

No matter how broken we may feel and no matter what has happened, God sees past brokenness to wholeness, because we are His children and He loves us. In His presence, what was stolen is given back. Like in the days of our youth, or as in the days when we first realized we were brought out of captivity, a song rises up at the realization of His restoration and love.

Because of Jesus Christ, when God looks at us, He sees His beautiful bride, holy and clean. These were the truths that I had to grasp in order for my own restoration in the area of sex and sexuality. God is the one who created sex and sexuality, and He is the One who can also restore it if it's been violated. As I learn more about God's love, His view of sex and sexuality, and through experiencing the healthy boundary lines of my marriage, my views of sex have been radically changed.

He also imparted the gift of discernment so that I could recognize the foxes, no matter the season. Discernment from the Holy Spirit can be especially heightened for those of us who have come out of any form of trauma, exploitation or addiction. Holy Spirit can help to discern spirits, even principalities, that are connected with addiction, lust, and the sex industry, including trafficking.

A Time and Purpose for Every Season

The whole earth revolves around seasons. We can learn about seasons in the scriptures and in relationship with God by His words spoken to us. Learning about the Israelites and how they journeyed from Egypt to the Promised Land also brings understanding. Being mindful of spring, summer, fall and winter, as well as the festivals according to the Hebraic calendar, can give us depths of insight towards understanding the seasons of life.

Like the butterfly goes through seasons of change to transform, so too, do we. There is an appointed time for everything. Written some time before his death, King Solomon authored Ecclesiastes. In Ecclesiastes 3 he writes:

> And there is a time for every event under heaven -
> A time to give birth and a time to die;
> A time to plant and a time to uproot what is planted.
> A time to kill and a time to heal;

A time to tear down and a time to build up.

A time to weep and a time to laugh;

A time to mourn and a time to dance.

A time to throw stones and a time to gather stones;

A time to embrace and a time to shun embracing.

A time to search and a time to give up as lost;

A time to keep and a time to throw away.

A time to tear apart and a time to sew together;

A time to be silent and a time to speak.

A time to love and a time to hate;

A time for war and a time for peace.

Greco-Roman or Hebraic

After the Israelites were led out of Egypt, one of the first things God told them was to look to the moon (not the sun as the Babylonians did) to know the times and seasons (see Exodus 12:1-2). The Hebrew lunar calendar is set differently than the solar, which is how the Gregorian calendar is set.

The Gregorian calendar as America and much of the world has adopted is derived from the Greek. The Greek mindset has emphasis on reason and logic, and while those things are important, the Hebraic mindset focuses on the rational and experiential, which is essential. What I love about the Hebraic mindset is that there is no division. For example, the Greco-Roman mindset believes a relationship with God should not influence other areas of life, whether it be business, sexuality, education or government (i.e. separation of church and state). In contrast, a person with a Hebraic mindset knows that a relationship with God influences all areas of life, including behavior.

The Gregorian calendar was named after Pope Gregory XIII who reigned over the Catholic church in the 1500s. The calendar was revised from the Julian calendar, which was itself a revision of the pagan Roman/Greek calendars.

When my husband and I were in Israel we learned more about the Hebrew calendar and the Jewish way of life, including many of the festivals because of the holiday season in which we were there. We also learned about *shabbat* - a time of rest beginning Friday nights at sundown that lasts until Saturday evening at sundown. This day to *cease* started at sundown, which according to scripture, is actually the time when each day begins. Saturday evening into Sunday would then be considered the first day of the week.

God's intention for sabbath has always been about rest, reading the Word, gathering with family and experiencing His presence in a sacred time and space. Jesus said in His very first sermon that *He* is the sabbath (see Matthew 12:8), and so it is in Christ, that we find shalom - complete wholeness and rest as a way of life in every moment of every day.

While in Israel, we noticed that many of the Jewish people stayed inside with their families on shabbat. Everything shut down in the community. Literally *all* of the shops closed. I recall being in awe when I saw that no one was out and nothing was open while walking with Corey from where we were staying. We learned to stay inside and take time with one another the following Friday, which is how our Fridays have continued ever since.

Typically for our night of rest, we disconnect from phones and television. Together, we spend time in the Word and with one another. We've also called this our date night. There are occasionally times this evening of ceasing does not happen. We are not religiously keeping shabbat (another term for rest), but we do enjoy and find great rest in honoring this set-aside time that God spoke of in His Word. When protecting this time of Shabbat, not only have we felt refreshing in our relationship with one another, but we've experienced a deeper devotion with God as well.

In addition to a seventh day of rest, every seventh year was to be a special sabbatical year in Jewish tradition. Every seventh cycles of seven years was followed by a year of ceasing, called a jubilee year.

There is blessing in cycles of seven.

Listed here are just a few of the Hebrew months. These are actually the months in which each season begins:

Month One: Nisan (March/April) Esther 3:7, Nehemiah 2:1
Month Four: Tammuz (June/July)
Month Seven: Tishrei (September/October)
Month Ten: Tevet (January) Esther 2:16

The Jewish calendar is based on three astronomical phenomena: the rotation of the Earth about its axis (*a day*), the revolution of the moon about the Earth (*a month*), and the revolution of the Earth about the sun (*a year*). The Torah designates the month of Nisan (scripturally called *aviv*, or *spring*) as the first month of the year (Exodus 12:2). This is not to be confused with the head of the year, Rosh Hashanah, which is celebrated in the seventh month, Tishrei. The beginning of the year then, actually starts around mid-March or early April, which here in the United States is spring. In contrast with the Gregorian calendar which sets the new year to start in January. Doesn't it just make sense that the start of the year would begin in the spring?

One of the reasons I love Minnesota is because there are very distinct seasons. It may be freezing cold or sunny hot. All things are in blossom after the winter and an array of color is displayed in the fall. There is a purpose for each season. What would spring be without the winter? What would the sunlight and clear skies be without the storms that have passed?

Here are the seasons related to some of the Jewish holidays:

Spring - New beginnings, blooming, refreshing, and coming alive. The spring holidays in the Hebrew calendar make way for a new season, preparing for Passover, spring cleaning, and a celebration of freedom as the Exodus from Egypt occurred in this time (see Exodus 12:2; Song of Solomon 2:11-12).

Summer - Hot and rainless (see Mark 13:28). A time for gathering and preparation (see Proverbs 10:5).

Fall - There is not mention of autumn or fall in scripture, however, fall is a time for planting and preparing for the winter. Times of harvest are also often associated with fall. The Jewish civil year begins in the fall and there are many holidays during this special time of repentance and celebration.

Winter - White snow is a reminder of washing and being found pure because of Jesus. Speaking out of a repentant heart David wrote, "Purify me from sin with hyssop, and I will be clean. Wash me, and I will be whiter than snow" (Psalm 51:7). White snow is a reminder of God's gift through Jesus Christ. Winter is also a time where it is more difficult to travel. We are given opportunities for rest and to stay in or retreat with loved ones. Winter season can come with anticipation.

In studying the seasons and learning from the Hebrew calendar, festivals and celebrations, I have found myself lining up with a rhythm that feels natural. Coupled with a study on the roots of the Gregorian versus the Hebrew calendar, comes the wisdom of getting in line with the Hebrew calendar and the rabbinical thought process. God has never based any of His works on the Gregorian calendar. He did, however, create the seasons in His infinite wisdom to teach us the lesson that He is in control of the time that events happen.

Days and nights revolve to the rhythm of the seasons. Seasons are defined by the movements of the master clock in the sky, and the master of that clock is God.

Scripture tells us, "He made the moon for the seasons; the sun knows the place of its setting" (Psalm 104:19). The seasons, including the moon and the sun, belong to God. It is time to watch the Hebrew calendar and get on God's time, the way He has told us. Even though we can be constrained by some of the same terms as the secular culture, there are ways we can live out the Hebrew way, finding a joy and natural rhythm that actually helps us to be focused.

Refining in God's Perfect Timing

One of my husband's favorite scriptures verses is Psalm 34:10, "The young lions do lack and suffer hunger; But they who seek the Lord shall not be in want of any good thing." Prior to resting on this promise for a wife, Corey went through a time where he thought his next next step after coming to Christ was to get married. God led him on a different path, a path of focus. After he got sober in 2004 and rested on the Psalm 34:10 promise, he stayed single. He didn't get sidetracked, but kept his focus on Christ. We met in the fall of 2008 and were married shortly after that time in 2009.

Becoming totally obsessed about the season we're in can cause unwanted anxiousness. It is God who has fixed the times and seasons in His own authority. He will bring them about in His own time and His own way. With a focus on Him, you'll recognize what the season is.

Take Peter for example. In the midst of waves from stormy weather, Peter walked on water while looking directly at Jesus. He was focused. It was the moment he took his eyes off Jesus that he sank (see Matthew 14:22-33).

Mary Lennox was so focused on finding the garden key that it didn't matter what people said to her. Even when she was told to forget about the garden, she knew in her heart it was destiny to find and cultivate a garden back to life. She wasn't about to let distraction throw her off the good path.

God taught me about His love in a season of singleness that I needed. As He drew me by His Sprit to focus on Him, He took care of the fox. Sometimes we get ourselves into our own messes when we focus too much on the wrong thing. It is those times when we must learn to take the actions that will bring about a good change. If nothing changes, nothing changes. We complicate a simple act of obedience.

My friend Marcus, also known as Tru-Serva, once said in one of his songs, "Two words bring change, trust and obey." He is right. If we refuse to allow the leading that comes with refining to change our actions, we will suffer the consequences. A hard heart is the result of someone not willing to follow the gentle, yet needed, leading of the Holy Spirit.

We each have a choice.

At the time of ending that relationship that I was being led out of, I felt torn, but if I hadn't followed the promptings, I wouldn't have grown in a season of needed singleness. I would not have met my husband, who God had in mind as a perfect partner from the beginning of time.

Whether it be a spring or winter season, a time to plant or to uproot, or even a season of singleness, focus can cause refining that aligns with God's perfect timing. Trust God in the refining. He "will send down the showers in their season; they shall be showers of blessing" (Ezekiel 34:26 ESV).

Take delight in the Lord, and he will give you the desires of your heart. (Psalm 37:4)

FOCUS KEY

Father God, thank You for love, guidance and focus. Thank You for the refining, of which, I welcome into all of me - body, spirit and soul. Give me dove's eyes for You. Reveal and deal with the foxes that come to ruin what is good in my life, and by Your Spirit, enable me with strength and wisdom to turn from those things. Thank You for strength and the continuous leading of Your Spirit.

In the name of Jesus, Amen.

1. What activities can you cultivate on a daily basis to keep your focus?

2. Although we do not want to focus on the foxes, it is good to identify them and set necessary boundaries. What foxes have you identified and what boundaries can you set?

3. What is your plan of action to set boundaries to protect your time with the Lord?

12

TIME TO RECONCILE

Therefore, we are ambassadors for Christ, as though God were making an appeal through us; we beg you on behalf of Christ, be reconciled to God.

2 Corinthians: 5:20

While caught up in the industry, heavy in a progressive and fatal addiction, I traveled home for a weekend in hopes to get away from it all. Home for me was the same small town where my sister and I had created our forts. Home was the same place where I had hidden the keys to my secret garden. Home was also the place where I was recruited and brought into the sex industry.

On one particular weekend, my loving mother mustered up all the strength she could find to pull me aside and say, "I don't want to lose you too." She proceeded to share information previously unknown to me. She told me that her sister once worked in a club as well. She was my mother's older and only sister, a talented artist, friend and daughter.

I never got to meet my aunt. Sadly, she tragically passed on at a young age. I never heard my grandma talk about her much. Perhaps it hurt too badly. I do remember seeing photos, which I adored looking at. My mom and her sister reminded me of my sister and I.

My dear mother had tears in her eyes as she told me she knew where I was and what I was doing. Thinking of me in the same place where her sister once was must have been heartbreaking. While I was caught in the web, I know my mom prayed often. God was at work to bring the message of reconciliation into our family, and not only through immediate family, but also through the generations, as well as those involved in the betrayal.

I remember my mother telling me about her sister and where she had once worked, but I did not leave the industry until several years later. After over a decade of addiction and almost six years in the industry, I hit the absolute rock bottom that my mother had been praying for. Every one of her tears and every word she prayed was collected and heard by God.

A plan was in place for not only redemption but for reconciliation.

In the midst of the mess, the ministry of reconciliation was in the making. The hearts of individuals would soon turn towards one another. When I finally got free, with God's heart turned towards me and my heart towards Him, I was able to learn love and honor for those around me, including my mother and those who brought betrayal.

In the great tapestry of life, from generations past, the power of reconciliation was woven into the storyline. Reconciliation is in all of our storylines.

Dreams for the Daughters

Fast forward to about a year after my graduating college to become a counselor, I continued to have dreams of the strip club.

No longer was I playing the seductive, entangled puppet that I once felt like. In these dreams I could see and hear all that was going on within the club. My focus in the dream was on the precious women. There was a growing desire deep in my heart to go back, but this time to build a bridge, and be the kind of love I had been encountering.

The Lord had been teaching me all along to learn to hear His voice, follow His lead and to also be spiritually discerning. After a needed time of healing and training, I would be going back into the club for the purpose of reconciliation as well.

Over time, the Lord brought together a small team of friends who, to this day, give their time to help put together gifts for those in club, including the managers and bouncers. If you recall the introduction, it was God Himself who brought the commissioning, gave the word and the keys. There have been times Holy Spirit has led us to go without physical gifts, but nevertheless, for His purposes. Through prayer and remembrance of my aunt Sandy, as well as my own journey, the name "Bella Daughter" was given for this outreach. The word *bella* means "beautiful." Bella is also short form of Isobel or Isabella (Hebrew), meaning "God's promise." The name in Latin means "battle."

With love motivating us to show honor, we go to war for God's daughters of promise right where they're at. A gift, just like a listening ear or the sharing of a testimony, is a demonstration of love. The desire to be loved and accepted is at the core of every single one of us.

I wonder how my aunt Sandy would have responded to a gift, a listening ear, or even a moment of prayer together in the club, had someone come to her with honoring love, understanding, and no condemnation.

The greatest of all gift-givers has it all figured out. He is a God of reconciliation who wants each of us to know how deeply we are loved. He desires for each of us to love one another with honor, which is what happens when we meet with the women in the clubs.

What a miraculous gift to partner with God as He works out love, grace and reconciliation through conversations and moments together with friends.

Reconciliation is Not Bound by Time

Reconciliation in light of the scriptures means we can have a restored relationship with God through Jesus Christ, thanks to His incredible gift. I believe it also means we can have restored relationships with one another.

Reconcile, according to the *American Heritage Dictionary* means:

1. To reestablish a close relationship between: reconciled the opposing parties.
2. To settle or resolve.
3. To make compatible, harmonious, or consistent: reconcile my way of thinking with yours.[6]

My mother and I needed restoration in our relationship, especially when I finally came out of everything. There were wounds I inflicted upon her, and wounds that were inflicted upon me - not out of intention, but out of our own hurts and deception.

In the restoration journey, my mother and I stepped into a ministry of reconciliation that would continue to bear fruit over the years. A ministry that can cause hearts to turn toward God is urgent and it is vital - it's truly a matter of life and death.

On the evening of an outreach night for *Bella Daughter*, my mother helped by putting a few gifts together. These gifts would later be given to the ones who were working at the very same club her sister once worked at. After getting all the gifts ready, we also took time in prayer. It was such a sweet moment.

Only God could orchestrate that!

Reconciliation was in the works, for "(He) gave us the ministry of reconciliation," and "we are ambassadors for Christ, as though God were making an appeal through us" (see 2 Corinthians 5:17, 20).

Each time I step into that specific club where my aunt once worked, it is love and understanding that I feel. The real gift is being able to hear the hopes and dreams, sometimes songs, and reality truths of what might be going on for someone. Had I been approached back in my time in the iron furnace, I wonder how I would have responded?

The fragrance of love draws attention from the heart of one who is ready to receive it, whether in a church or in a strip club.

Hope can move through the generations of time, riding on the wings of prayers and of love itself. A man named Jesus laid down His life in love, and His love *never* fails.

And what a comforting truth that love never ends!

The love that my mother has for me, and that I have for her, never ends.

The love that God has for us never ends.

Another comforting truth is that there is grace in mistakes. *Grace* means "to receive something that you do not deserve" or "unmerited favor." God is abundant in grace, not that we go on making intentional mistakes. We are being refined. His greatest act of grace is the gift of salvation that is available for each one of us by faith (see Ephesians 2:8-9). When the gift is accepted, eternal life is promised to the recipient. Eternal life is a promise of a home one day in heaven. Here are a few of my favorite verses on grace:

Thus says the Lord, "The people who survived the sword found grace in the wilderness - Israel, when it went to find its rest." The Lord appeared to him from afar, saying, "I have loved you with an everlasting love; Therefore I have drawn you with lovingkindness." (Jeremiah 31:2-3)

Therefore let us draw near with confidence to the throne of grace, so that we may receive mercy and find grace to help in time of need. (Hebrews 4:16)

And the Word became flesh, and dwelt among us, and we saw His glory, glory as of the only begotten from the Father, full of grace and truth. (John 1:14)

God is not restricted by time, so neither is grace or reconciliation. Yes, there are consequences to our choices, just as when a seed is planted there is a healthy or unhealthy plant depending on the kind of seed sown as well as the soil in which the plant grew. We can step into the design of a good Father who is in the business of reconciliation, which means the consequences of our actions can meet with grace. Even the seeds sown in generations past can yet be redeemed.

Love has caused me to sow healthier seeds, thoughts, words and actions. Thank goodness He's not done with me, because I'm still a work in progress.

I have to believe there is rejoicing in heaven when my amazing mother helps put together gifts that later go into the hands of God's beautiful daughters in the clubs. Each time one of His daughters experiences His love - a kind of love that reconciles, forgives and brings about reconciliation - there is rejoicing.

Prayers Answered

Back then, on that weekend I came home for a break, my mother had an understanding of what was going on. Each time I called her, which wasn't that often, it was a time I needed comfort. Just hearing her voice helped soften the reality of what life had become. Years after my leaving, she told me she was praying for me one morning. She knew where I was working and that I was involved with an abusive man. As she prayed one afternoon, her attention was drawn to a young deer that was actually swimming across the lake outside the back of the house. The deer was struggling to get across the lake, swimming frantically with its head just above water.

It is not a usual thing to see a deer swim all the way across a lake. This was an odd moment, but a sign as an answer to prayer. As she watched the deer make its way to shore, the Lord reminded her of me. Although I was struggling, looking as though I was going to drown, God was going to pull me through to the other side - from Egypt to the Promised Land.

In Romans 8:28 the scriptures states "...God causes all things to work together for good to those who love God, to those who are called according to His purpose." When the choice is made to turn to God or to forgive, reconciliation covers the wounds of generations. Remember, "Love never fails" (1 Corinthians 13:8a). The ministry of reconciliation has been committed to us in relationship with Jesus Christ, meaning He very well may be making His appeal of love through you, even if it's difficult.

Courageous Forgiveness

In the fall of 2015, my mom and I went to the place where my aunt Sandy was killed. My brave mother stood in the place where tragedy had happened decades before. God's hope was experienced in the moment that we stood in silence to honor Sandy's life.

Not only did that day bring us to a location, but that day brought us to the house of the man involved with her death. Before getting out of the car to speak with the man, who was standing outside of his house, my mom listened to a significant story that Corey wanted to share with her.

Corey's dad was killed in a car accident when He was just a teenager. For years he held onto hate. He even turned away from God in anger and professed atheism in the depths of alcohol addiction, which never did drown the pain of loss. It wasn't until He encountered God's love and was later led to forgive the man who crashed into his dad's car that he was able to heal and not be angry anymore.

Hearing that story gave my mom courage to do what only Holy Spirit could do through her, with her partnership of willingness.

The moment we got out of the car, he walked towards us. This was the man who was excused from a long prison sentence, which I know made things all the more difficult for my mother's family.

Standing there in front of that man, my mom and I stayed close together. For strength, we held each others hands as she looked him in the eyes. After a few words were exchanged, she looked at the man and said, "I want you to know I forgive you." I'll never forget the look on his face. He cringed in a moment of remembrance. Even so, some kind of love entered into his heart.

Even more amazingly, my mother had just stepped further into the reconciliation that would release love and forgiveness for not only herself, but for the generations to come.

Anger and bitterness are deadly. These toxic thistles can creep into the generations to cause patterns of sickness and addiction unless they are dealt with through the love of Jesus Christ, who is Himself reconciliation. Forgiveness does not make right what the other person did. Forgiveness allows love to flow through the hearts of both the one betrayed and the betrayer. Haven't we all in some way brought betrayal in thought, words or actions, and been betrayed?

In the winter of 2018, I came face to face with the man who had lured me into his body, black spirit and raging soul of lust. It had been eleven years since I saw him. During a Holy Spirit infused counseling session years past, I had a vision of Jesus being there to lead me out of that moment of violation and every other moment in that coat closet or entangled in the web of that club.

In that God ordained moment, we looked at each other face-to-face. I had been nervous, but knew that it was time. The last two days prior to our meeting had been spent not only encountering the love of God, but also spending time with others who, like myself, had at one time been caught up in the trap of Egypt. Prayed up and ready to move with an army of warriors, I walked back into that club, knowing I would see him. This was actually the fourth time I'd been back in that place and not one of those times did I see him until this night. God had been preparing me and He knew in my heart I had already forgiven that man.

Because Holy Spirit dwells on the inside of me, I know that he encountered some facet of Holy Spirit. This was a moment of surprise, healing, forgiveness and awakening. He said my name - not my old stage name, but my first and last name - maiden name and all. I too, called him by his full, God-given name.

God sees you and He loves you. He is drawing you out with awakening - out of the web, and into His Kingdom. He created you with a destiny and a purpose and this is not it.

That night, I had the most amazing experience of healing. I also had an intense dream of intercession where I saw that manager encountering not only the love of God, but an opportunity to repent and walk away from the web.

The true enemy, satan, wants to continue destructive family patterns. Because the blood of Jesus Christ speaks a stronger message, generational patterns that cause tragedy and violation can come to an end. God is at work to bring the message of reconciliation to family, and not only through immediate family, but also through the bloodline of generations, as well as to the one who brought violation. The question is, will the one who is caught up recognize the significance of God's love in this hour of urgency? Will there be a turning away from what entangles?

Family trees, which include family patterns, are very important to understand. Behavior and health problems can repeat themselves through the generations unless otherwise addressed. Forgiveness, even if there has been no apology, brings reconciliation.

We can forgive because He forgave us.

We can have beauty for ashes and gladness instead of mourning, because we were created for a love that never ends by a God who is Himself, Love.

> Giving them a garland instead of ashes, the oil of gladness instead of mourning, the mantle of praise instead of a spirit of fainting. So they will be called oaks of righteousness, the planting of the Lord, that He may be glorified. (Isaiah 61:1-3)

RECONCILIATION KEY

1. Have you seen the gift of reconciliation within your family or relationships, and if so, how?

2. Write out the different scripture verses based on grace and reconciliation.

3. Was there anything that you were reminded of as you read this chapter?

13

ADONAI, EL-ELOHE-ISRAEL

The Lord is a warrior; The Lord is His name.

Exodus 15:3

Two years after going to Israel, as I prayed and pondered, Holy Spirit reminded me of all the incredible things that happened while my husband and I were there. Memories filled my mind as I recalled our feet on the same ground, in the very same places where Jesus once walked.

Pressing further into prayer, I was led to ask God, "Who are You?"

A gentle whisper of Holy Spirit answered, "I am the God of Israel."

Song erupted and words began to flow. Immediately, I was reminded of the purposes of our Israel visit: healing, vision, equipping and *to bless Israel*. To be in relationship with God is to love, align with, and bless Israel.

And I will bless those who bless you, and the one who curses you
I will curse. And in you all the families of the earth will be
blessed. (Genesis 12:3)

When God made a covenant with Abraham in Genesis 12:3, He
was not only referring to Abraham as an individual, He was also
referring to Abraham's descendants. These descendants are the
Jewish people and those of us who are grafted in. We are all
partakers of the promises and inherit the blessings of God's salvation. Therefore, we are to not only bless the physical nation of
Israel in the Middle East, but we are to also bless and pray for all
Jewish people to acknowledge Jesus Christ as the Messiah, the one
true Messiah that He is.

A Battle of Sounds

Waking up in Nazareth, my husband felt well rested after
sleeping soundly through the night. I had gotten very little sleep,
but nevertheless gathered my things in a rush to be ready to board
the bulletproof bus. The night before, I had spent time in prayer,
declaring Psalm 91 over us as I listened to gun shots going off just
outside our door. When you're on the night watch, like I often am,
that's just the way it goes sometimes. Prayer in the midnight hour is
an aspect of awakening. My midnights now look a whole lot
different than they once did.

In Israel, during that last week of September 2015, I become so
irritated by the sound that was blasting over the loud speakers each
morning. Trying to quickly get ready so we wouldn't miss our bus, I
asked Corey to join me in prayer while also telling him about the
urgency I felt in my spirit for a new sound to be heard.

From the depths of my spirit came forth a declaration that a
new sound would be broadcasted into the air instead of what we
were hearing each morning. Anyone who has been to Israel
knows what I am referring to. To bring understanding, I'll say we
were all hearing the sounds of worship to a different god every

morning over the loudspeakers. I do not know what was being prayed, but I do know it caused me to feel a weight that came with confusion.

Corey and I stood outside on the balcony and in unity we declared that a heavenly sound would come forward to honor and worship the one true God of Israel. I clearly remember being led to say that a new sound would be broadcasted. Now, keep in mind, this was all Holy Spirit-led. Holy Spirit moves within us to bring divine alignment with God's plans and purposes. In turn, God the Father gets the glory.

Once we returned from Israel, through the leading of the Holy Spirit, I stumbled upon a video published online the first week of October 2015. One week after our declarations, a Jewish man decided that he too, was sick of the same sound. He thought it was time for a new sound to come forth through those loudspeakers, and that's exactly what happened.

Standing on top of a building with his loud speakers and sound system, he broadcasted a new sound into the air. He sang some of the words of *Shema Yisroel,* a call to prayer that came with the name of God as Adonai. *Adonai* is the Hebrew name for God meaning "Lord" or "Master." If God is Adonai to you, He is the one to whom you submit or bow down; He is the good leader of your life who leads you towards what is best.

A journey of restoration comes when we follow Adonai's leading. We learn to build new altars of praise, even when it's difficult. The Jewish man had heard enough of the sound that did not give honor or praise to Adonai, so he did something about it. He broadcasted a new sound in reverence and honor of El-Elohe-Israel, The God of Israel. In essence, he built an altar through his actions and songs.

Understanding Altars

Noah was the first person recorded in scripture who built an altar. After the flood, he wanted to give praise to God because he and his family had been protected. He acknowledged that the God of Israel was his protector.

An altar is a place of sacrifice and worship. A biblical image for worship, or an altar, in the Old Testament was a significant aspect of a visible devotion to God. Typically, an altar was a raised up platform on which a fire was kindled. Sometimes actual rocks were gathered together to make up this place. Altars would be placed in the open, where the scent of the sacrifice would reach the heavens. Remember, life is found in the blood, which is why in the old covenant animals were sacrificed as a means of atoning for sins. In the new covenant, we know that it was Jesus who died as the perfect sacrifice. He is the Lamb of God who shed His blood for the sins of humankind.

Another place in scripture where we can read about an altar being built is after Jacob cried out to God for deliverance from his brother Esau. The altar Jacob built also came after he literally wrestled with God for a blessing. In Genesis we read: "Now Jacob came safely to the city of Shechem, which is in the land of Canaan, when he came from Paddan-aram, and camped before the city. He bought the piece of land where he had pitched his tent from the hand of the sons of Hamor, Shechem's father, for one hundred pieces of money. Then he erected there an altar and called it El-Elohe-Israel" (Genesis 33:18-20).

Being victorious after the struggle in which Jacob received the new name "Israel," he built his first altar there in Palestine. His altar was dedicated to, "El, the God of Israel." Just like Noah built an altar when he came into a new land, so too did Jacob. They both built an altar to worship God.

The word worship is from the Hebrew verb *shachah* which means "to bow down."

The heart is an altar that can not only give honor and praise, but which can submit (or *bow*) to the leading of the one true God of Israel who leads us by His Word, Jesus Christ, and the Holy Spirit, who is the best Counselor.

. . .

Mount of Olives

Currently, access to the Mount of Olives is difficult unless you hire a taxi to take you up, or the Lord provides you with a tour guide who knows how to get there. Our guide was an amazing Arab Christian man who knew a lot about where to go and how to get there. Getting connected with him was a miracle.

During that particular day in Israel, I needed to get away from the crowd, and God knew it. We had been praying for a way to visit the Dead Sea and the Mount of Olives and God sent a man who took us to both. We were able to go from the low place (the Dead Sea), to a high place (the Mount of Olives) with freedom of time. This led to destiny moments and building a new altar that also brought healing.

While on the Mount of Olives, the man guarding and caring for the prayer house led by Tom and Kate Hess allowed us to come inside. Although a large group from the convocation had just left, he let us come in where we were able to spend time not only in prayer, but also in worship.

In that prayer room, a place positioned in the heart of Israel, I sat down at the piano. Thoughts of Jesus flooded my mind. The top of the Mount of Olives is where He will someday stand.

> In that day His feet will stand on the Mount of Olives, which is in front of Jerusalem on the east; and the Mount of Olives will be split in its middle from east to west by a very large valley, so that half of the mountain will move toward the north and the other half toward the south. (Zechariah 14:4)

A new sound erupted from my womb. An altar of praise was built and a new sound was released as my prayer momma and I prayed. Playing a few notes paired with the sound of our voices, we worshiped King Jesus there, in that place. I realized there was some kind of fulfillment of restoration for me in that moment. I remembered a dream, some moment in time that was being played out, in which I would sing for healing. There was a deep connection with God the Father, through Jesus Christ and Holy Spirit.

Moments of *deja-vu,* "remembering something as though it has happened before," that come with vision, in an honoring love, are from God. This was one of those moments.

Before leaving the Mount of Olives, we spent time in prayer that came with gratitude. This was a time that had been orchestrated for restoration somewhere in the timeline of God's perfect design. To worship Jesus in that place brought the arukah kind of restoration that only an encounter with Holy Spirit can bring. *Arukah,* a Hebrew word from Isaiah 58:8 means "healing, restoration, health, perfected, restoring to soundness, and wholeness."

God brought me into a new land, Israel, so that I could further heal from the wounds of Egypt. There, we blessed Israel and Israel was a blessing to us.

Vision of Hannah Mei

Also in Israel came a vision of destiny for the future, because of grace.

With the vision came the needed healing from the deceit of the past to know that I could be a mother. The memory of the one whose name is known in Heaven and in my heart would not be a secret anymore because what happened on June 27 of 2001 was not the end of the story. While I was yet healing and gaining hope for things to come, Corey was given a vision of a little girl of Asian descent. As he decreed the vision, tears flooded my eyes and hope grew in my heart. As God was teaching me about altars, a new sound, and healing, He was also preparing us for adoption.

The Altar of the Heart

Access to God has always been through an altar - not the altar of material, but the altar of the heart. An altar is built as a symbol of a place of sacrifice. In the New Testament, this corresponds to our praise and worship that we express to God.

> Through Him then, let us continually offer up a sacrifice of praise to God, that is, the fruit of lips that give thanks to His name. (Hebrews 13:15)

Praise can flow from our entire being - body, spirit and soul. In the first book of Peter we are told:

> You also, as living stones, are being built up as a spiritual house for a holy priesthood, to offer up spiritual sacrifices acceptable to God through Jesus Christ. (1 Peter 2:5)

Today, we build an altar to the Lord by becoming a living, walking, talking likeness of Him. By sacrificing selfish wants (what we think is best), we instead can follow His perfect leading.

God, the God of Israel, continues to draw each one of us into the fullness of restoration, as we are told in Philippians:

> For I am confident of this very thing, that He who began a good work in you will perfect it until the day of Christ Jesus. (Philippians 1:6)

In the waiting of refinement and fulfillment of promise, God is removing the names of the false idols from our mouths. Not only are we beginning to see clearly what these false idols are, but we are also being awakened to tune our ears to God's strategic sound that orchestrates an army to move in unity.

BLESS ISRAEL KEY

1. What Scriptures can you find that support the significance of blessing Israel?

2. Identify and write out different biblical stories that have to do with altars.

3. According to Hebrews 13:14-15 how can we give praise to honor God?

4. According to 1 Peter 2:5 how can we worship God?

Declaration:

In the name of Jesus Christ, I bless and speak peace to Israel. May revelation understanding come that Yeshua is the One True King, the Messiah.

In Jesus name, Amen.

EPILOGUE

In an awakening, not only does the shoe fit, but the Bride of Christ becomes a warring bride who can sing and dance in the throne room. She can also step on the serpent with her combat boots and kick down doors of bronze as she sings, *"Adonai ish milchama!"*

Continue to unlock the garden with keys of truth in Volume 2 of The Garden Keys, 22 Keys of Restoration. In this real-life journey towards freedom, hope rises even from the depths of grief stemming from a long kept secret. Journey from trauma to triumph with keys of truth to enter into the fullness of restoration - body, spirit and soul.

The final key of restoration is the greatest key of all. Along the way, become tuned into the *best* sound as you prepare for the *greatest* dance.

You were in a field wearing this gorgeous white dress, almost like a wedding dress. And you were twirling with such freedom. All of a sudden, the picture faded. When it became clear again, you were dancing, but this time not as free, and the dress was a little frayed and torn. All of a sudden, Jesus came towards you. He began to dance with you. At first, you wouldn't look at Him, but then He took your face in

His hands and gazed into your eyes. When He did, your dress became white again and it was like new.

Shake yourself from the dust, rise up, O captive Jerusalem; Loose yourself from the chains around your neck, O captive daughter of Zion. (Isaiah 52:2)

ABOUT THE AUTHOR

DANIELLE FREITAG, LADC serves as the co-founding director of Action169. An overcomer of severe addiction and the commercial sex industry, Danielle works as a counselor and advocate, providing direct support, care and counseling for women in a variety of settings. She is the creator of Arukah, a trauma-informed, faith-centered counseling service promoting holistic restoration through evidence-based practices, including the creative arts. Her mission is to empower women to overcome substance use and to enable those in the strip club industry to know their intrinsic worth.

Offering expert training on combatting the realities of exploitation and addiction while providing best care practices, Danielle has been requested to advise medical, government and non-government professionals and churches, both nationally and internationally. Danielle's captivating story of transformation inspires hope and offers solutions.

Corey and Danielle met in the fall of 2008 and were married shortly after, in 2009. The two have had practical and theological training and equipping to provide care services for youth and adults facing challenging life circumstances. In their free time, Corey and Danielle love hiking, traveling and helping others live a healthy lifestyle. They are known for their passionate love of God and desire to carry the message of the good news of Jesus Christ. They reside in Minnesota and serve in leadership positions in ministry as well as throughout the local business community.

ACTION169

Action169 is built on a foundation of prayer and is committed to ending commercial sexual exploitation and substance use through Christ-centered prevention, intervention and holistic restoration care services.

For speaking inquiries, to host *The Garden Keys* workshop, or for more information on Arukah restoration counseling services, visit the Action169 website.

Action169.com

Info@Action169.com

Bella Daughter

Bella Daughter is an outreach of Action169, a survivor-led organization. Bella Daughter's mission is to love, support and empower women in the sex industry to know their intrinsic worth.

BellaDaughter.com

ABOUT THE ARTIST

Art has been and continues to be an integral and vital thread inter-woven into Anna Friendt's personal story and life journey. It has been a God-given gift that the Lord has used to give her hope from her past and has enabled her to share that same hope with others. God has used artwork in Anna's life to assist in the process of breaking free from depression and anxiety and has provided her a way to heal from a traumatic childhood as well as a troubled young adult life.

Anna uses her work to display Truth. Art is a gift to be shared, which is why she founded *Anchor 13 Studio* - a collaborative studio with a mission of pointing the hearts of people towards the same kind of healing and restoration that she has been able to experi-ence. She is passionate about bringing artists and nonprofits together to promote heart healing and restoration.

Anna's personal artwork can be found via her personal small business, Anna Friendt Artwork & Illustration.

For more information on Anna Friendt please visit anchor13studio.com.

Book Endnotes and Permissions

1. Chapter 2, page 26: 2006, *The Yale Book of Quotations* by Fred R. Shapiro, Section: William Ellery Channing, Page 143, Yale University Press, New Haven

2. Chapter 3, page 34: *The American Heritage® Dictionary of the English Language*, Fifth Edition copyright ©2017 by Houghton Mifflin Harcourt Publishing Company

3. Chapter 7, page 84: 2013, *Prayer: Why Our Words To God Matter* by Corey Russell, Page 37, Forerunner Publishing, IHOP, Kansas City

4. Chapter 8, page 101: 2013, *Prayer: Why Our Words To God Matter* by Corey Russell, Page 53, Forerunner Publishing, IHOP, Kansas City

5. Chapter 9, page 112: 2006, *Dream Language*, by James and Michal Ann Goll, Pages 28 and 29, Destiny Image Publishers INC, Shippensburg, PA

6. Chapter 12, page 160: *The American Heritage® Dictionary of the English Language*, Fifth Edition copyright ©2017 by Houghton Mifflin Harcourt Publishing Company

For more info on the Hebrew word definitions and usage found throughout this book, please see The Hebrew-Greek Key Word Study Bible, NASB Revised Edition ©1984, 1990, 2008 by AMG International, Inc.